sportsproview

DEATH OF A FOOTBALL CLUB?

The Story of Cork City FC – Season 2008

by Neal Horgan

Print edition

Published by *sportsproview*

www.sportsproview.com

© Neal Horgan 2014

ISBN 978 0 99306 220 9

To my mother Mary, my father Pat and my uncle Martin

CONTENTS

Preface

"Those who cannot remember the past are condemned to repeat it."

George Santayana, *The Life of Reason*

The passing of time has brought many changes to football in Cork. And yet as the old adage goes: the more things change, the more they stay the same. From an early age I had a desire to learn what had become of the football clubs that had previously represented Cork in the League of Ireland. Perhaps I had more reason than most.

My maternal grandfather, Jackie Lennox, enjoyed a very successful period as a tricky left-winger with Cork Athletic in the 1950s, and was later involved as a director with a fabled Cork Hibernians team of the 1970s – the demise of which ultimately led to the promotion of the Marina-based Cork side Albert Rovers to the League of Ireland in the late 70s and early 80s. My father, Pat, and my paternal grandfather, Paddy Horgan, were deeply involved in 'Alberts' as player and chairman respectively. And later, in 2001, Jackie Lennox's son – my uncle, Brian Lennox – would assume control of Cork City FC, further consolidating my family's connection with Cork football.

Unfortunately I never really had the opportunity to ask my grandfathers what happened to these clubs, and my father never seemed interested in talking about what had caused their disappearances (the loss of the iconic ground, known as 'Flower Lodge', to the Gaelic Athletic Association was a topic best avoided). He preferred to talk about great players and dramatic victories – and who could blame him? He wanted to encourage me to stay in the game; the details of the decline and demise of those once-treasured Cork clubs were not for my ears.

My mother offered more information but not quite enough to satisfy my curiosity, so I was reduced, in pre-internet days, to scouring dusty scrapbooks that had been meticulously put together by unknown figures in my extended family. I found 'financial difficulties' mentioned in some of the newspaper pieces, but the main articles, cut out and stuck onto the pages, were inevitably more concerned with legendary victories.

I would later learn that there had been many other Cork clubs, of whom I'd never even heard, in the League of Ireland throughout the 20th century. There was Fordsons FC (the first club to represent the county), which was created in 1924 and made up of workers from Henry Ford's famous car and tractor factory. There was a tremendously successful team called Cork United in the 1940s; a Cork Bohemians; and an earlier (though short-lived) Cork City FC. In all, something in the region of eleven clubs have represented Cork in the League of Ireland to date.

So what happened to these clubs? Why did they fall from the league? What must it have been like for their players and fans? Could their difficulties have been avoided? To this day I've never really discovered the answer to any of these questions.

So in the summer of 2008, as a player at Cork City FC, having learned that the club was going through 'financial difficulties' I decided to document as much as I could of the experience.

The result is this book.

~

Chapter One

Glory Days

I still feel aggrieved that I wasn't at the match that day. Cork City playing Bayern Munich in competitive European football, a mere five minutes from my house. And to make matters worse, in the lead-up to the game German international Stefan Effenberg had told the media he was positive they'd win, and that City's star midfielder Dave Barry looked like his grandfather. (Unbeknown to Effenberg, Barry was a particularly talented and combative dual star – he'd won Gaelic Football All-Ireland titles with Cork in 1989 and 1990 – and was not one to underestimate. Effenberg, who went on to captain Bayern for the Champions League title in 2001, had made a serious error.) The whole city awaited Barry's response, but none came before the match.

"They're winning, they're one up – Dave Barry scored!" my 19-year-old sister, Tara, proclaimed with delight as I came in from school.

It was rare to see my sister delighted about anything, let alone a football match. I was trying to come to terms with this glorious update when my thoughts moved to my brother, Eoin. At 15 (four years older than myself), *he* was the one that would be the most interested – the most aware of this game's significance. I couldn't wait to tell him that Barry had scored. So where was he?

'Me and Eoin' had been there together in the hard days, dragged along by our dad to the cold, wet, muddy banks of Turner's Cross. We were at 'the Cross' when City only needed a draw against Dundalk to win the League (I can still hear the silence that descended when Dundalk scored); we were in Dublin at Lansdowne Road against Derry when Dave Barry hit the post, allowing a famous Derry team to win the treble; we were there when our dad's team – University College Cork, which he managed – got to play at the Cross in an important local cup final, and lost. We'd endured the heartache of those days – the type of heartache only young fans can endure. As far I could see, my sister had never been too bothered. Now here she was, standing over the radio, taking over the whole thing. Where the hell was Eoin to put her in her place?

Then all the bad news came at once.

There was the hint of a smile on her face as she delivered the first blow: "Daddy and Eoin are at the match."

Within minutes Effenberg had equalised for Bayern.

I can't say there weren't tears and recriminations, but we rallied together in the end, my sister, my mother and I, to cheer City as they held on.

UEFA Cup: 18th September 1991, Musgrave Park, Cork

Cork City 1–1 Bayern Munich

Later that evening my father and brother returned home in buoyant form. After a word from my mother, however, they assumed a more restrained mood and made a combined attempt, in the upstairs bedroom I shared with Eoin, to explain the treachery. I sat on the bed and listened attentively while my father, a barrister, led the talking and Eoin nodded seriously alongside him. Clearly this was a routine that had been rehearsed.

The early kick-off, combined with the fact that Eoin had been on a half-day (it was a Wednesday and he was at secondary school) were the main reasons proffered. Unfortunately my young mind couldn't accept the logic in this.

"I've missed Cork City draw against Bayern Munich," I submitted. "This will never happen again. Never."

They ran into some difficulty attempting to counter my point.

(Three years later my father would bring me to the US to watch Ireland in the second round of the World

Cup against Holland. There was no mention of the Bayern match, but I sensed the trip was an attempt to settle matters. Ireland played poorly, lost the match and were knocked out of the tournament. This I didn't mind. My problem was that Eoin was there too.)

~

Cork lost the second leg in Bayern 2–0, but a mark had been made. Even the BBC and Eurosport were impressed by the "plucky part-timers" from Cork.

Of course, like every other kid in my park, I followed Gaelic Games and Irish rugby at certain times of the year; yet for me Cork City FC was capable, every now and then, of offering something very different. Apart from their usual challenge to the near-permanent Dublin hegemony that exists in the Irish domestic league, for a week or two every few years in European games they became David versus Goliath. They were not only up against some top European side or other: they were challenging the established order of things – taking on history and the rest of the world.

Two years after the Bayern match, City were again up against one of the more familiar European names and, older and wiser, I was going to be there to see it. This time it was the European Cup proper, and City – having triumphed in their first-round match against Welsh opposition – were drawn against Galatasaray of Turkey. A respectable 2–1 loss in Turkey (with Barry scoring again) had left the tie very much in the balance; the return leg would be played at City's new ground in Bishopstown, which had been bought and developed by then-chairman Pat O'Donovan, who had ambitions to move the club forward. It was the first time the club had owned a ground.

A full house of up to 10,000 people turned up, including myself and Eoin. City held their own well into the second half and the excitement was palpable around the ground as we watched them begin to turn the screw on the Turks. Then all of a sudden came the shouts: "He's in, he's in!" and the stadium lit up.

Anthony Buckley, City's young winger, was played through with just the keeper to beat. The crowd fell silent as he took his shot, and then Eoin and I cheered and hugged, along with the rest of the crowd, as the ball hit the net. I felt relief – the hurt of the Bayern treachery leaving my soul.

But no.

"Stop – get off me!" said Eoin, "It's only the side netting."

The Turks soon broke away and scored. The dream was over – for another few years at least – and the heartache returned.

European Cup: 15th September 1993, Bishopstown, Cork

Cork City 0–1 Galatasaray (aggregate 1–3)

Move forward ten or eleven years. Skip past a financial near-meltdown after the Galatasaray match, and the takeover of the club by a group of local businessmen including future chairman Brian Lennox.

Fast-forward through a restructuring of the club and the emergence of a talented team under Dave Barry (as manager), and disregard their near-title-winning seasons – for now, at least.

Skip to Turner's Cross in 2004 and a leaping Kevin Doyle at the back post, so far off the ground I could only stare in amazement. City were playing Dutch side NEC Nijmegen in the second round of the Intertoto Cup, and this time I was closer to the action. Having made my way into the first team squad a few years previously, and then broken my leg in a recent league match, I was sitting in the stand with crutches by my side. The team had knocked out respected Swedish club Malmo FC in the first round, and then held Nijmegen to a 0–0 draw in the first leg of the second, and the place was buzzing with talk of this new City side.

Brian Lennox had personally taken the reins of the club and was keen to progress it further. He'd hired the colourful and passionate Pat Dolan as manager – which was quite some meeting of minds. Both wanted full-time football for the club; both were sceptical of the influence of English football in Ireland; both were ambitious and hungry. For a while Dolan's infectious enthusiasm and grand plans were sufficiently backed by Lennox. A full-time squad was assembled for the first time in the club's history, including future Irish internationals Doyle and Shane Long. There was a sense of expectation that had not been felt around City for some years.

The Dutch, when they emerged onto our little ground at Turner's Cross that day, all looked six foot plus. I remember one of their players looking up at Doyle, bemused, as he hovered a good metre above for a second.

Then the crowd erupted. It was in the net and Doyle spun away in celebration.

Intertoto Cup: 11th July 2004, Turner's Cross, Cork
Cork City 1–0 NEC Nijmegen (aggregate 1–0)

I was sitting in the stand, still with my crutches, a
few weeks later when FC Nantes came to town for the
second leg of the third round tie. The French had won
the first match 3–1, but our away goal had given us a
fighting chance.

To the overwhelming delight of the Turner's Cross
crowd, Doyle scored and we needed just one more
goal to go through. The feeling seemed to spread
around the ground: we could do it. We could be the
first Irish team to qualify for the group stages of a
European competition. But, alas, the French broke free
to score late on, and the dream had to be postponed
once more.

Intertoto Cup: 24th July 2004, Turner's Cross, Cork
Cork City 1–1 FC Nantes (aggregate 2–4)

A year later things really started to heat up within
the club. Dolan departed following a dispute with
Lennox, and Damien Richardson (Rico) came in for a
second stint at City, having previously managed the

team in 1993/94. Dolan had made the players fit and ready; Rico, when he came in, was like a grandfather to the lads, guiding us reassuringly to the top end of the league. He had the artistry and assurance to apply the finishing touches to a team primed for glory.

The European games arrived. We beat a Lithuanian side – FK Ekranas – in the first round relatively convincingly. In the second we were drawn against the soon-to-be Swedish champions Djurgårdens. The first leg was played at their National Stadium, and with 10,000 to 15,000 people the ground was half full. It was my first big European game and the sun was in my eyes as I got the ball from the kick off. The natural League of Ireland tactic would've been to launch it into the corner, but no – they'd dropped off, far off. We had time on the ball, time to knock it around at the back. Lovely stuff.

The only problem was that once we went forward and lost the ball we didn't get it back for five, maybe ten minutes. That's ten minutes of chasing, hurrying after your marker, organising those around you. Hard work.

They knocked it around us comfortably, and then their wingers made sudden darting runs behind us. We, the fullbacks, had to cover the runs... but the ball wasn't played: they kept it and went back to the other side of the pitch. Then they came back over to my side and their winger again sprinted like a madman, attempting to get played in behind me. Swedish internationals Tobias Hysén and Mathias Johnsen were manning the wings for Djurgårdens, but my fellow fullback Danny Murphy and I held tough, as did our entire team. Again and again I sprinted to cover a run from Hysén. There was no let-up; it was concentrated, drilled possession. A grinding of the opposition – constantly probing and testing while keeping the ball all the time. I had never experienced this in the League of Ireland.

The Swedes, fortunately, didn't have enough to break us down, and in the second half our distinguished forward Neale Fenn made the breakthrough with a goal. Fenn had spent his developing years at Tottenham Hotspur and his class really shone through against Djurgårdens. He looked the most comfortable with the ball being kept on the ground (rather than being sent high and forward to chase, as was the norm in Ireland and the lower English leagues) and he guided our team through the tie. Everything went through him; he held off their players, turning, swiveling and controlling the ball simultaneously.

The Swedes put us under severe pressure towards the end. I was nearing exhaustion, having matched Hysén's sprints. They finally scored late on, but we took a respectable draw back to Cork.

UEFA Cup: 11th August 2005, Råsunda Stadium,
Stockholm
Djurgårdens 1–1 Cork City

We packed the Cross for the return leg, 7,000 or so squeezing into our stadium. The atmosphere was intense and it seemed some of their players were even intimidated by it. We played conservatively but effectively, holding on after a late push by them.

UEFA Cup: 25th August 2005, Turner's Cross, Cork
Cork City 0–0 Djurgårdens (aggregate 1–1)

For the second year running we'd knocked out a Swedish club in Europe. Now we were in the serious end again – at least for us. We drew the Czech side SK Slavia Prague in the third qualifying round, with the winners to progress to group stages. No Irish side had ever made it to the group stages of a European competition. This was real history-making stuff; I could hardly bear the excitement. Unfortunately the added pressure proved too much for Rico and he suffered a stroke (he still managed to get in on the action, however, by being interviewed live at half time from his hospital bed in Cork...).

After 15 minutes on the pitch in Prague I could tell I wasn't going to have a good day. My head was in the clouds – dark clouds. I had a nightmare. Their left-winger terrorised me from start to finish. Our keeper Michael Devine had the game of his life to give us a small chance in the second leg, but even so we lost 2–0.

UEFA Cup: 15th August 2005, Stadion Evžena Rošického, Prague

SK Slavia Prague 2–0 Cork City

I felt mortified and exposed. What had happened to me? On the flight home my mind, well versed in self-defence, desperately searched for answers.

A few days later, back at our training ground in Bishopstown, I cornered our sports psychologist and we went through some of the things that might have affected my performance. I formulated a substantial list. Perhaps it was the live TV, being broadcasted back to Ireland, that had unsettled me. Or was it the presence of the unusually large group of friends and family that had travelled to Prague to see the match?

Was I thinking of them? Maybe it was the dead leg I had been carrying and trying to ignore. Or how about the absence of Rico? Perhaps it was none of the above and merely an experience I needed to go through as in any workplace; a baptism in European football – if a particularly brutal and painful one.

For the return leg in Cork, Rico, now discharged from hospital, told us to leave nothing in the dressing room. We tried to intimidate them, to outmuscle them. But they were too strong.

Even so, we were climbing fast.

UEFA Cup: 29th September 2005, Turner's Cross, Cork

Cork City 1–2 SK Slavia Prague (aggregate 1–4)

The humiliation I experienced in Prague served me well for the rest of the season; I took lessons from it and vowed never to leave myself exposed again. I knew any thoughts that could get in the way of my performance had to be put aside if I wanted to avoid that gut-wrenching humiliation. I would have to be prepared – completely prepared – for every match, and be on my toes at all times. It was as though I'd been exposed to a poison: I'd suffered, but my defences had been rebuilt and were now stronger than ever.

I believe this is what happens when a player or team is exposed to a superior opponent (in football or any other sport); they suffer through it and (hopefully) come out the other end better informed. I knew what it was about now, and I was ready.

For the rest of the season I worked harder than ever before, as did the entire team – and on a memorable November night in Cork, on the final day of the season, we beat Derry to win the League.

League of Ireland: 18th November 2005, Turner's Cross, Cork

Cork City 2–0 Derry City

A few weeks later, on a cold, horrible night in Dublin, we missed out on a rare double at Lansdowne Road, losing to Paul Doolin's Drogheda United in front of 25,000 fans.

FAI Cup Final: 4th December 2005, Lansdowne Road, Dublin

Drogheda United 2–0 Cork City

In 2006, however, as league champions, one of the biggest shows in the world awaited us: the Champions League. We couldn't wait to hear the music as we walked out ('*the champiooons, dun dun dun den*').

When it finally came around we won our first match in Cork against Cypriot team Apollon Limassol, with Billy Woods scoring a screamer. Then we went through in Cyprus thanks to a Dan Murray header, although a chaotic punch-up following the final whistle left two of our best players – Joe Gamble and Danny Murphy – suspended for the following round.

Champions League: 19th July 2006, Tsirion Stadium,
Limassol

Apollon Limassol 1–1 Cork City (aggregate 1–2)

We now faced another renowned European team in the form of Red Star Belgrade, with the winners set to play AC Milan in the final qualifying round. It didn't take long to figure out who I'd be marking should we proceed to the final knockout round: Kaka, current World Player of the Year. Glorious stuff indeed. But shortly after hearing that music again as we walk out in Cork, our striker Denis Behan scored an own goal and we lost the first leg at home 1–0.

Champions League: 26th July 2006, Turner's Cross,
Cork

Cork City 0–1 Red Star Belgrade

A week later I was comfortable and confident in Belgrade. I no longer felt inferior; I didn't care about the TV or the travelling fans and was in the best condition of my life. But as a team we had not improved. With a side weakened by suspensions and other factors (including the recent loss of key players to clubs in Dublin and the UK) we lost heavily.

Champions League: 2nd August 2006, Stadion Crvena Zvezda, Belgrade
Red Star Belgrade 3–0 Cork City (aggregate 4–0)

In the dressing room afterwards I felt frustrated and upset. We should have given them a better game. We should have gotten close – maybe even beaten them. They weren't, I felt, as good as Slavia Prague. Something had gone wrong and our upward curve was beginning to level off. It was frustrating because at 26 I felt I was in the shape of my life. I had been exposed to European competition at a high level and wanted more. I *needed* more in order to continue to develop – but maybe that was not to be.

We returned home and finished a disappointing fourth in the League. We lost more key players to UK clubs, without bringing in any clear replacements.

The next year, 2007, Rico made some important signings to replace the departures, including two former Irish internationals, Colin Healy and Gareth Farrelly. But neither could play for a few months due to a new UEFA three-club rule. Then Rico and one of our main players, George O'Callaghan, had a falling out and George soon moved to a club in the UK. The team languished in or around fourth place again for the season, comfortably away from the leaders. In Europe, after overcoming Icelandic opposition in the first round of the UEFA Cup, we were knocked out without much of a fight by Swedish team Hammarby.

UEFA Cup: 14th July 2007, Råsunda Stadium, Stockholm
Hammarby IF 1–0 Cork City (aggregate 2–1)

About this time Brian Lennox, realising he could push the club no further, found investors who seemed eager to pump money into the club. They were initially fronted by a Canadian named Jim Little, and later by a Corkman named Aidan Tynan. There was an element of secrecy about the whole thing, yet the name 'Arkaga' seeped out into the public. It became clear that Lennox would remain on the board for a year as acting chairman to help oversee the transition, but Arkaga now ran the show, and there was a feeling around the place that they weren't great fans of Rico.

FAI Cup Final: 2ⁿᵈ December 2007, RDS Arena, Dublin

Cork City 1–0 Longford Town

In a wet and windy RDS we finally won the FAI Cup, Denis Behan making up for his OG against Red Star by scoring a diving headed winner. However, all was not well and everybody could feel it. Rico was under pressure from the new owners – in fact we all were.

Chapter Two

Dolan and Rico, 2003–2007

Pat Dolan, on his arrival as manager of CCFC in 2003, had reorganised the club root and branch – paying particular attention, initially, to the public relations aspect of the job. The local papers were immediately impressed by his presence and drive – and, most importantly, by the results. He was full of charisma and brought a certain razzmatazz to a club that seemed to have travelled over a desert of dullness – a trip that was led by Dolan's predecessor, Liam Murphy.

Murphy had sacrificed popularity for principles; without fanfare he'd implemented sustainable practices at the club. He was later judged by some to be negative and unimaginative (traits that are often the hallmarks of a manager who plots a steady path through a difficult period). His reign happened to coincide with a changing of the old guard, and upon inheriting great players near the end of their careers he decided to keep them at the club for as long as possible. He knew how much the young local players (author included) could learn from these older guys, whose once-shining lights were beginning to fade. In this way Murphy actually laid the foundations of our League win in 2005: he signed six out of the starting eleven that played against Derry to win the 2005 league.

But when Dolan arrived with all that razzmatazz, Murphy's contribution was deemed old-hat. It wasn't long before some very astute free signings, coupled with an expensive purchase or two, brought the club to dizzying heights. However, the main impact of his arrival, for me, was the realisation that we had turned into an athletics club.

The Mardyke athletics track in the city was to prove a popular spot with Dolan. He liked to occupy one particular end of the track, and players would run significantly faster as they approached this end. We knew we were being watched – every muscle twitch, every breath. Fitness tests at the University of Limerick, under his dementedly driven eye, became tortuous for many. If Dolan deemed you unfit for his team, or his plans, he treated you with contempt. He had an obsessiveness about the job that has been unmatched by almost any other manager I've worked with.

He monitored what the players ate and drank; on one of our earlier fitness adventures I spotted him leering at me across two tables as I ate one of the apple pies that had been served to us. His look I understood immediately. Recent tests had revealed that my body-fat percentage was higher than that of most of the other players, so, for Dolan, my decision to eat this pie constituted a breach of trust. In order to resolve the situation he took to following me around shops and restaurants on away trips. I was not alone in this: others, with similar body-fat readings, were followed too. Poor little Liam Kearney, just signed on his return from Nottingham Forest, was caught bringing a packet of 'Burger Bites' crisps onto his first trip away with the team. Dolan made him suffer.

On European trips we were under his unrelenting control for three or four days straight. We evolved a strategy of chartering any willing – and often innocent – smuggler to set out from our hotel in search of sugary foods. Standard smuggling terms applied: if caught, you were on your own. Denis (Behan) was nearly lost forever when one such venture turned ugly: caught red-handed in the foyer of the hotel, the players' pain on seeing the bags of chocolates and sweets fall into the hands of Dolan and his cronies was substantially mitigated by possession of a beautifully remote vantage point. We giggled, sensing the slaughter of a player who, having also signed recently, was going through a ridiculously loud and indecipherable phase (Denis has a strong accent originating from the Kerry/Limerick border) with most of us. But, as we would all learn on later occasions, Denis has hidden depths of character – and cuteness – and he remained coy. He said he was "unaware" of the rules as he was new to the group. Dolan appeared enamoured by this smart reaction – the reaction of a streaky striker, perhaps – and Denis was spared... for now.

Prohibited substances under Dolan's regime included soft drinks, white bread, chocolate, crisps, chips, fried food and alcohol. He was, of course, correct and forward-thinking in this approach, but his methods of enforcement were to prove excessive. He would roam the city in his car, looking for players who might stray. Some players claimed they had strong evidence that he'd engaged various informants within the publican and bouncer trades. He famously arrived into one drinking session that the lads were halfway through and ordered a round of water to be brought to their table; on inquiring as to who'd ordered the water the players were pointed to the shadowy figure of Dolan in the corner.

Midfielder-come-striker George O'Callaghan recounts an episode where he was enjoying himself in a nightclub only to see Dolan wading his way through the bodies on the dance floor towards him. George was accosted, and then escorted through the nightclub and out into Dolan's car and taken home.

Like many managers, Dolan chose to talk up close to you on weekend morning sessions, and any suspicious smell could mean trouble. Blood tests were instigated on at least one occasion.

Pat fell out with me for two weeks after he'd driven past me and I was drinking from a can of Coke. I hadn't seen him, and it took him a few days to explain why he was upset with me.

He would often call into the lads' houses unannounced and go through their fridges and cupboards in search of prohibited goods. The unlucky player would tell the rest of us the following morning in training and we'd listen in disbelief. "*Ding dong...* who the hell could be calling at this hour?"

Pat.

He'd put his head into the fridge and angrily throw onto the floor items that were not allowed. I made a point of not telling him where I lived.

"Did you eat your broccoli, Hoggie, eh? Eh?" he would often taunt me in a semi-humorous way in front of everybody during pre-match meals. But there was fierce intent underlying the humour. He was obsessed with making us a professional full-time team.

Other changes that he made in this regard included the arrangement of pre-match meals before home games; players were asked to be at the hotel for 4pm instead of arriving at the ground for 6pm; more and more training was arranged; you had to bring your own water bottle (with your name on it) to training; you had to arrive early – at least thirty minutes before training. The players with demanding or inflexible day jobs away from football soon fell by the wayside. The majority of the older players left at this stage too. It was very clear we were only going one way: towards full-time football, Dolan-style.

While the discipline that he was instilling was a positive development for the team, away from the pitch he also seemed to want full control over every minute of our lives. "It's how you live your life," was one of his loaded sayings.

Regular, random body-fat tests were introduced at training. Everything was noted down and analysed. We seemed to be training every night, running and running in the dark, and Dolan seemed to be waiting around every corner, shouting and encouraging but also judging. We soon became very fit.

As well as the increase in frequency of training, the sessions also became longer. Set pieces, corners and free kicks became central drills; we spent an incalculable amount of time standing around listening to him tell us what to do. A centre-back in his playing days, preparation of set pieces was one of Dolan's main strengths, in my opinion, as a coach. He would make us practise over and over again, corner after corner, free kick after free kick. We'd practise defending free kicks with a wall. He'd choose who was in the wall, and then he'd get Denis – who has a freakishly powerful shot – to hit the ball at the wall, over and over. The players had to stand there and get hit. It wasn't fun, but it worked.

He also insisted on playing infuriating games in training: not good old open five-a-sides, but games with conditions such as two touch forward, one touch back. His overall philosophy was to control the way we played from above.

He had brilliant catchphrases that he used during training – especially in his early days – and they improved the whole experience. "Make your touch golden!" he would shout as we took the ball around a training pole; "Beautiful!" he would declare if you did something well. He insisted that I had the skills of a Brazilian, which was a nice thing for him to say and it made me feel special.

He made funny little jokes during stretching times before and after training. He invented a stretch where you leant forward and pushed your legs back into the air, and he called it 'the Hoggie' (after me) for some reason. "Do the Hoggie with the Max Bygraves hands!" he would say, shaking his hands. There was also a Colin T. O'Brien stretch: "The 'T' is for terrific," he would insist. Then there was the stretch he named the 'shake and vac', which he claimed would "put the freshness back, lads."

Despite his extreme ways he was genuinely funny and charismatic, and not long into his reign the place seemed to lift up into the sky. He was demanding excellence but promising trophies and fame.

Every week we seemed to have new trialists training with us. They'd come from anywhere on Earth. Dolan would treat them real well until the trial was over, and if they signed they were his. Mind, body and soul. All forms of freedom would be severely restricted.

The day of a match under Dolan always involved meeting ridiculously early. We once met at midday for a 7.45pm match in Waterford – which was only an hour-and-a-half's drive away.

At about 4.30pm, after pre-match, he would make a speech that he'd prepared using a flipchart. He spoke passionately and was often very funny. After showing the teamsheet he'd reveal a new image every week on the flip chart; it might be a kid-style drawing of a flight of stairs, and he would ask us what was going on.

"We're climbing the stairs," we'd answer, and he'd smile and giggle like crazy.

The next week it might be a picture of a phone, drawn with red marker. It'd be ringing. "Answer the call," he'd say, laughing, before turning deadly serious: "That phone is ringing – are you going to answer it Hoggie, eh? Are you, Danny?"

It amused the lads. Then, to end each session, a new page would be revealed showing a sketch of a circle divided into four quadrants. There'd be a letter in each quadrant representing the initials of Cork City FC. Players were chosen by Dolan to come up and write out, using a marker, what the CCFC stood for. He wanted us to write Calm, Committed, Focused and Controlled; he wanted us to know the right words and exactly where they belonged. Every away game this would happen, three or four hours before the game.

He was extremely well informed about the opposition. He would tell us which of their players had been out drinking during the week; he would tell us which player was having a problem with their manager, which had had a fight with his girlfriend or was looking for a move. Whenever we were in a position to judge this information it always seemed to check out. He seemed to be permanently in the know, and this intensified the control – both real and imagined – that we felt he had over us.

Before matches he could be inspirational. He would literally be jumping about the place, hands clenched and arms bent like a boxer protecting his chest. There was no doubt he was fully committed; it was clear this meant everything to him.

When you were in his favour – when things were going well for you – he made you feel as if you could take on the world when you walked out the tunnel.

After a while we noticed that he had an unusual superstition: just as the whistle was blown for kick-off he'd walk up to the half-way line, just off the pitch, and move first to the left and then to the right, kicking each foot out as he did so. Then he'd jump up twice and do a 360-degree neck roll before leaning forward, clapping a few times and going back to the dugout. It was always the same, every game. It's revealing that we didn't think too much of it at the time – we just accepted it as another part of his inspirational, if a little crazy, jigsaw.

Sometimes the passion would spill over and he'd lose the run of himself during matches. After a bad pass he'd jump up to the sideline, crouch, and shout and shout. Again: jump, crouch and shout. If you were a full-back, like me, and he was jumping up and down next to you, it was hard not to let it affect you. If it was you he was shouting at it could be frightening.

But he tried to be positive, he really did. On the good days he'd shout, "Well done, Hoggie!" or "Brilliant!" or "Hoggie – tell Benno to tell Murph well done." He'd make sure we got the message across to the other side of the pitch, which sometimes caused a bit of head-scratching.

But there was the darkness in him too. He could treat people very well and very poorly in the same day. He had his favourites, and they could change. Another of his sayings – one that would only emerge after a poor result – was "There'll be changes," which was a clear threat to everyone. You became dependent on remaining in his good favour. Things were particularly miserable if you weren't in the team, as this meant more running and more training and more looks of disdain from Dolan.

On the pitch, though, the improvements were very evident. We finished third in his first season (2003) and then second in 2004. But in the background his relationship with chairman Brian Lennox had broken down, and one afternoon a few weeks into the 2005 pre-season it emerged that Dolan had been sacked.

As is so often the case in the changing of a manager, the players were divided about whether this was good or bad news. Some were genuinely upset; others were genuinely thrilled. The latter group had grown tired of his repressive policies, and I have to admit there was some relief on my part.

My relationship with Dolan over the two-and-a-half years that he was manager at the club was, for the most part, the same as that of my teammates. It could be defined as love-hate. He loved you when you played well – and you were truly delighted and boosted to feel that you were part of his ambitious plans – but if you played badly, or were at fault for a goal, it was as if you'd insulted the man's wife, and no amount of effort in training during the week could fix it. If he wasn't happy with you it was personal and only a good performance the following week could ease things. When you were out of favour you could expect to be judged unfairly in training matches; he'd find fault where none existed – on purpose or not, you didn't know. But you could see there was some method to it.

However, for me, at least, it increasingly became all stick and no carrot, and my situation was not helped by Dolan's falling out with Lennox. Lennox –

as Dolan well knew – was my uncle, my mother being his older sister, and around this time I sensed a growing distrust from Dolan towards me. Our relationship became strained. There were no more comments about my being like a Brazilian, and 'doing the Hoggie with the Max Bygraves' was rarely mentioned. There were a number of other indicators too, and overall I felt things were getting progressively worse between us.

While a breakdown in relations between a player and a manager often happens in football, in this case I was unhappy with the source of the problem between us. So I decided I'd have it out with Dolan face-to-face. One morning before some PR event (we were always doing PR events) I told him how I felt – how I thought his situation with Lennox was affecting the way he was treating me. He responded by telling me I was imagining it.

In any event I wished we could just get on with things as normal, and to an extent we did. Having broken my leg in 2004 I made my way back into the team and we went on a winning streak. Things were OK again; and we looked forward to 2005 with genuine hopes of silverware.

But then he was sacked.

I felt bad for the guy: Dolan had obviously had a huge impact on the club, boosting it in countless ways. I cherish many memories that were fundamentally of his making. But while I wasn't happy he was out of a job, I'll admit I'd had enough of some of the madness.

I felt like I'd just stepped off some gameshow – a gameshow that had slowly taken over my life. It had been a perverse mix of *Big Brother*, *Catchphrase* and *Weakest Link*. In truth I was glad that it was over and I could get my life back. I wanted to get back to enjoying football, the simple game, without the gameshow elements.

Despite this, I, along with my fellow players, had undoubtedly benefitted from the Dolan era. By the end of 2004, due mainly to Dolan, we had a large, talented and fit squad carefully poised to challenge on the domestic scene as well as in Europe.

When Dolan left, things were unsurprisingly not the same. In fact the difference between Dolan and Rico couldn't have been starker. Rico was philosophical and laidback; he wanted us to trust ourselves – he believed the key to a successful team was trust. He wanted players to be happy because only then would they play to their best. His training involved uninhibited five-a-sides.

He believed in rest as much as training; he believed that one of the main benefits of becoming full time was the opportunity to rest more often as well as train more often. If you played badly he'd approach you the next day and have it out with you, and then it was over – you could move on. Next week was a fresh game and last week's was left behind.

You didn't have to be watching your back in shopping centres and restaurants; you could go back to the rest of your life and not worry too much. He was older and more patient than Dolan.

In his first year we won the League. It was amazing. Two weeks later we lost the cup final, missing out on a rare double, and over the next two seasons we lost player after player to Dublin and the UK – and they weren't really replaced. We finished fourth in 2006 and fourth again in 2007. And even though we won the FAI Cup that year, Arkaga were not overly impressed.

Towards the end of 2007 Rico was criticised by some fans for allowing complacency to set in following the 2005 league win, to the extent that they accused him of turning Cork City into an 'also-ran' outfit. The Arkaga board seemed to share this view; it fitted with the general idea that Rico was easy on players – that players under his watch could do as they pleased. While this was basically an unfair appraisal, there could be said to be some merit in it, particularly if Rico's approach was compared – as inevitably it would be – to the madcap ways of his predecessor.

Arkaga brought Alan Mathews in for 2008, but by this stage Dolan and Rico had done the business.

Chapter Three*

Pre-Season and Early-Season Form, 2008

*In this chapter the extracts shown in italics are taken from '*Season Preview 2008: Cork City*', written by Turlough Kelly and published on www.extratime.ie, 21st February 2008

If every season gets the cup final it deserves, then the 2007 FAI Cup decider couldn't have been more representative of the seismic disruptions which have altered the landscape of domestic football ever since the FAI handover. A Cork City side whose management and playing staff appeared in open revolt against the club's new owners (whoever they were; nobody seemed quite certain on that score) lined up against an already-relegated Longford Town, managed by the heir apparent to the soon-to-be-vacant Cork throne.

As ever, football (or something resembling it) triumphed over the backroom machinations for ninety minutes at least, as Denis Behan's 60th-minute winner earned Cork their second FAI Cup in the windswept and inhospitable surrounds of the RDS. The bubble of jubilation was pricked even before the medals had been draped over the winners' necks, however, as Cork captain Dan Murray provocatively characterised the victory as "two fingers to the board" in an on-field interview with RTÉ.

Dan Murray's live comments after that cup final in 2007 were, understandably, not well received by club CEO Aidan Tynan and Arkaga. But the fact that the majority of the squad shared Dan's sentiments would soon become clear during the post-match bus journey from the RDS to our upmarket Dublin hotel.

Players were busy celebrating an historical second FAI cup triumph. Champagne and beer were in ample supply; songs were being sung. It was all fun and games, until a chant started up: *sack the board, sack the board, sack the board...*

While this was greeted by laughter in most circles, it soon became clear that we'd caused some discomfort for people sitting at the top of the bus. I saw some shuffling and head-turning, and before long Brian Lennox – still the acting club chairman – rose from his seat and walked down towards the back of the bus.

A hush fell over the players. Lennox spoke with restraint, simply asking us to have more respect for the people on the board, including himself. The players respected his request, letting him know it wasn't him we'd been singing about, but Lennox was clearly still unhappy.

"You must show respect to everyone on the board and everyone on this bus," he said. At which point, fortunately for all parties, the bus reached the hotel and off we went into the glorious Dublin night.

Not long after the cup celebrations had died down, it was reported on local and national media that our manager, Rico, had reached agreement with the new owners to leave the club.

A little over two months later, the discord has abated, the indignation has subsided, and all again seems relatively rosy in the Cork camp. Richardson was indeed outmanoeuvred and eventually dislodged (albeit after an agreed settlement) by the club's new owners (the Arkaga investment fund), who reportedly offered former manager Pat Dolan a generous financial inducement to again seize the reins which were dashed from his hands by the ancient regime. After apparently being rebuffed by their preferred candidate, Arkaga turned to Alan Mathews, manager of relegated Longford; a marginally less divisive appointment than that originally conceived.

[...]

Whether or not General Manager Aidan Tynan's grandiose vision for the club comes fully to fruition, Cork City will begin the 2008 season with a stronger and deeper squad, a new and methodical manager, a renovated stadium and a more stable atmosphere than the club has enjoyed for many years. In a city whose footballing narrative often mimics the sinuous course of the River Lee which winds through it, however, nothing is ever that uncomplicated.

The Manager
Something of a surprise appointment to the position, Alan Mathews has demonstrated a remarkable ability to pilfer silverware with limited resources and limited players. How he adjusts to the very different challenge of managing a major club with serious expectations will define his premiership. With a generous three-year contract nestling in his desk drawer and a sizeable transfer budget at his disposal, Mathews will be judged by very different criteria to those which applied at Longford.

[...]

Taking charge of Longford in 2002, Mathews steered the unfashionable Midlands club to FAI Cup triumphs in 2003 & 2004, the latter of which was accompanied by victory in the League Cup. [...] The bubble finally burst in 2007, when Longford were relegated largely because administrative shortcomings had incurred an (ultimately fatal) six-point penalty. An exasperated Mathews took his leave of the club after leading them to the FAI Cup final, whereupon he succumbed to Arkaga's melodious overtures without much need for persuasion. He will be accompanied in the Cork City dugout by former Limerick 37 manager and Irish international Paul McGee.

"I'm absolutely delighted to be here, Neal," were Mathews' first words to me, shaking hands, upon his arrival into Bishopstown.

During the first few months I was greatly impressed by his hunger for this new challenge, and by his rational and modest personality. The new and returning players came and settled in quickly. Mathews organised a hard pre-season with his assistant Paul 'Skee' McGee, letting us know he had ambitions to win silverware in the year ahead.

Skee was to prove a popular character at the club. Bald and stocky in appearance, he'd played as a free-scoring centre-forward in clubs throughout Ireland, the UK and Europe in his day, and had famously garnered Diego Maradona's number 10 jersey when playing for the national team against Argentina. So he had the respect of the lads. As is the way with most assistant managers, Skee was in a position to be more friendly and popular with the players than the actual manager, and he was also always on hand to dispense a wealth of footballing advice to us young pretenders.

Such advice could range from golden nuggets of genius to blatant superstitions of idiotic proportion – and it wasn't always easy to discern one from the other. For example, Skee would insist that the best way to 'wear-in' a new pair of football boots was to get into a hot bath wearing nothing except the boots. I'm still not sure about that one. But if there were any doubts among the players regarding his advice, there was no doubting his fabulous ability to name coaching drills and passes after chocolate bars. (The 'curly wurly' was my favourite of these.) McGee, true to the role of an assistant manager, brought some much-needed light relief to training.

Pre-season with a new manager can be a time of great uncertainty for a player; you have to do everything you can to try and impress the new boss. Even if you've been in the team under the previous manager, you're now under review by someone new. You can lose everything you've striven to achieve on the whim of a new coach if he doesn't quite fancy you. Equally, if you've been on the fringes of the team or on the way out of the club under the old boss, this is a new chance – a blank page. The influx of new players also brings its own apprehensions, both for them and for the established core. In many ways all bets are off and everything's up for grabs.

Prior to this year, at least in the time I'd been at the club, the lack of other premier division teams in the Munster area – coupled with the inability or unwillingness to play Dublin clubs – meant that pre-season at Cork City often involved fixtures that lacked quality. The incumbent Cork City manager could then feel, with some justification, that a bad start to the league campaign was attributable to such pre-season constraints.

However, Mathews, with the considerable backing of the new owners, could have no such complaints in 2008. At the beginning of 2008 we were flown to Spain for a week to play in a pre-season competition in which Dynamo Kiev (and a few less notable European teams) were involved. The set-up was first class and seemed to serve as further confirmation to the players that the club was on the rise. Previous to this, in my experience, the furthest we'd travelled for a pre-season camp was two hours down the road to Tralee.

The Squad

As was frequently observed throughout the 2007 season, Cork City's first XI was as strong as any in the league. Unfortunately, Damian Richardson was seldom in a position to field such a team, and Cork

suffered as a consequence. With the purse-strings
loosened for new manager Alan Mathews, that
problem is unlikely to recur in 2008. Already,
Mathews has enticed play-maker George O'Callaghan
back to the club from a short and typically torrid spell
across the Irish Sea with Ipswich Town and Brighton
& Hove Albion. Joining him in the Cork attack will be
Dave Mooney, whose remarkable and unprecedented
feat of topping the scoring charts with nineteen goals
despite representing a relegated Longford team
alerted a battery of clubs in Britain.
[...]
Neither the goalkeeping nor full-back positions
give any cause for concern (in goal, the eminently
capable Mark McNulty will continue to deputise for
Mick Devine, and Pat Sullivan has joined from
Longford to provide competition in the full-back
slots), while the midfield engine room will be fiercely
stoked by Joe Gamble and Colin Healy. Billy Woods
and Colin O'Brien have both agreed to defer their
respective retirements for a further season and will

provide valuable and versatile support, particularly if Liam Kearney fails to awaken from the torpor which afflicted him for much of 2007.

As the season progressed it became clear that the ever-increasing professionalism at the club was leading to the marginalisation of the remaining part-time players, Colin T. O'Brien and Billy Woods. Both had been long-term servants of the club, but neither were to feature much in the early season. Colin soon decided to go on loan to Cobh Ramblers in order to get game time, while Woodsy spent most of his time in the first few months playing for the reserves. Admir Softić, a Bosnian who had featured prominently the previous year (most notably in a man-of-the-match display against Red Star Belgrade), flew back to Bosnia to play with a team there. About the same time a promising young player named David Meyler was sold with little fuss to Sunderland for a six-figure sum, having made a handful of first-team appearances at most.

Prospects

Despite an impressive injection of talent in the close season, Cork continue to look a number of key personnel short of a championship-challenging squad. With Drogheda, Bohemians and St. Patrick's Athletic having strengthened considerably over the winter, Cork would appear (alongside Derry City) to occupy the second tier of Premier Division contenders. There is, however, no lack of experience in the squad and progress from a relatively innocuous Setanta Sports Cup group should be assured (although Mathews' previous excursion in Europe do not augur well for the club's UEFA Cup prospects). Cork's season may hinge on O'Callaghan's re-integration into the team and Dave Mooney's ability (or otherwise) to rediscover his goalscoring form of last term. Under Mathews, solidity should be assured; creativity could take a little longer. Third place and another cup winners' medal to supplement his impressive collection is probably the best the new manager can hope for.

Our early-season form in the months of March and April (the League of Ireland season running from March to November) was anything but consistent. This may have been due to the changes in staff and personnel that had taken place since the previous season. We had problems winning games and seemed to be giving away last-minute goals every week, which infuriated Mathews. Video analysis was brought in on a more regular basis than before to help us identify and address what was going wrong. Around this time Mathews also decided to bring in a 'four-game plan', whereby we would all agree on a number of points that we felt were ambitious but achievable over the next four games. Mathews would write the agreed figure on a flipchart in the dressing room and it would remain there for the duration of the four games in question.

Crucially, he also offered an incentive of our choosing, should we achieve the desired results. After very little debate a unanimous decision was reached: a night away for the lads. Mathews happily agreed to this, perhaps safe in the knowledge that until this point we hadn't been able to put two straight wins together. Almost before the paper was dry on the agreement we set off on a fine run of ten league games unbeaten (from late May to the start of August), winning eight and drawing two. Mathews, elated at this turn of events, was true to his word and our night out was planned for later in the season.

It seemed we'd turned a corner. We were marching towards a challenge for the league title. But despite this, as is usual with such a large and talented squad, there was some unhappiness and a few clashes of personality among the playing staff. In fact, two of the new signings were to leave quite soon after their arrival. Unfortunately George O'Callaghan, who had been truly phenomenal for us in 2005, couldn't find the same form on his return from the UK; he seemed unhappy to be playing on the wing, with Joe Gamble and Colin Healy holding down the central midfield spots. At some stage Mathews and George agreed that it would be best for him to leave, and he made a move back across the water to Tranmere Rovers. At about the same time, Dave Mulcahy left after a dispute with Mathews in the dressing room while we were away to Sligo.

It was also soon clear that Mathews and Gareth Farrelly did not see eye to eye; for whatever reason, they seemed to disagree about most things. Such is often the way in football clubs, and had they been given time maybe things would have improved between them. Unfortunately, before this could happen, fate played its hand. Sometime over the summer Farrelly made a trip home to his family in England and didn't return to training the following Monday. News finally filtered through to us that he'd suffered a life-threatening aneurysm and was very fortunate to be alive. Obviously this meant he would miss the rest of the season, and as it turned out he'd played his last game for CCFC.

Farrelly, famously, had kept Everton in the Premiership on the last day of the 1998 season at Goodison Park with a fantastic half-volley from his unfavoured right foot. He had his detractors among our fans, but they were never on the receiving end of a pass of exquisite beauty from his left foot.

The main reason I'd enjoyed playing with Farrelly was because he had a positive effect on my performances; over the years I've learned that, in general, a right-back (such as myself) will receive more of the ball, further up the pitch, from his central midfielders if at least one of them is left-legged. This is because it's more natural for a 'left-legger' to find an advanced right-back with an attacking pass than it is for him to find his left-back. (This is, of course, not so much the case when the midfielder is facing his own goal.) With Farrelly in the side I had the advantage of knowing, before setting off on energy-sapping runs up the pitch, that he could effortlessly and consistently find me anywhere on my side of the field and – if my legs could get me there – behind the opposition's left-back. And he could do this from deep in our own half.

Therefore his ability changed my game; I suddenly became more attack-minded, happy to make deep runs that, if seen, I knew would be well fed. Farrelly's loss went unnoticed by some but not by me; the most talented players can raise other players around them without fanfare.

Off the field, too, there were changes of personnel. Club CEO Aidan Tynan, who had been most vocal in regard to the new owners' ambitions, stepped down from the job in April and was replaced by Dubliner Pat Kenny in mid-July.

By the end of July, following our ten-game unbeaten run, the team was in second place in the league and had emerged as serious contenders for the title. We were fast approaching a crucial clash with leaders Bohemians in Cork, but before we could focus on that we had to fly to Finland for the return leg of our UEFA cup tie against Finnish side FC Haka.

We'd drawn 2–2 in Cork against Haka and, having dominated that match, were hopeful of progression to the next round. As a further boost, just before we boarded the plane to Finland, the highly prized midfielder Joe Gamble signed a new three-year deal with the club. The future seemed bright.

Chapter Four

1st to 31st August 2008

'*Examinership* is the process whereby a company is placed under the protection of the High Court. The company is protected from creditors for up to 120 days. An examiner is appointed whose job is to consider whether it is capable of rescue and, if so, to bring forward a set of proposals for this purpose, known as a "scheme of arrangement"'.

(*Irish Times* special report on insolvency and recovery, 27th March 2009)

Friday 1st August

Heads are down as we arrive back into Cork Airport from Finland. Despite fielding a strong team we've been annihilated 4–0 by a side that had looked very average in Cork when we drew the first leg. The hammering is a glimpse back to the dark days of part-time football, when we were often soundly beaten even in the very first rounds of Europe. But this time we don't have any excuses. We were simply outplayed – particularly after Denis Behan received a red card for foul-mouthing the referee. Denis says he just reacted with a "for f***'s sake" to get his second yellow; how the Latvian ref understood Denis I'll never know, as the rest of us struggle to understand him at the best of times.

Waiting around the baggage conveyor at Cork Airport, nobody wants to look anybody else in the eye. Everyone's thinking the same thing: *just get me home*. There's a sense of shame.

A dejected Alan Mathews calls us all together just before we leave.

"Lads, the football side of things I'll leave for another day, but I want to talk about something else for a minute.

"Some of you might've looked at your accounts and noticed that the wages aren't in yet. The club wanted me to let you know that it's just a delay, due to some technical reason, and they'll be there by Monday or Tuesday of next week. So just go home, get some sleep and I'll see you all Sunday morning, bright and early."

The wages issue barely raises an eyebrow among the battered and bruised playing contingent who, still despondent after the match, swagger off out of the airport, gearbags over shoulders, into the night.

Sunday 3rd August

We're under intense pressure to react positively today. We're away to Sligo – a tough trip at the best of times. Fortunately Denis scores a lovely header to get everyone's heads back up.

League of Ireland Premier Division: The Showgrounds, Sligo
Sligo Rovers 0–1 Cork City

We've now won eight and drawn two of our last ten league games. Quite a run. So perhaps Finland was just a "once off", as the Gaffer keeps saying. Anyway, I'm happy with the result and with my performance. While it's pitch dark outside as we travel down the west coast of Ireland towards home, inside the bus there's a warm glow of satisfaction. Everyone's laughing and joking, and underlying it all is a feeling that we're back on track. We might be out of Europe, but we're really motoring up the League table.

League of Ireland Table, 4th August 2008

		Pld	W	D	L	Pts
1.	Bohemians	19	14	4	1	46
2.	St. Patrick's Ath.	21	13	6	2	45
3.	Cork City	21	12	6	3	42
4.	Derry City	21	10	7	4	37
5.	Drogheda United	19	9	4	6	31
6.	Sligo Rovers	21	7	7	7	28
7.	Shamrock Rovers	20	7	8	5	29
8.	Bray Wanderers	21	7	4	10	25
9.	UCD	21	2	8	11	14
10.	Galway United	21	3	5	13	14
11.	Finn Harps	20	4	2	14	14
12.	Cobh Ramblers	21	2	5	14	11

Friday 8ᵗʰ August

Still no sign of our wages (which are supposed to be paid fortnightly on a Friday). The Gaffer spoke to us again yesterday and explained that the money was due to be transferred into our accounts today. But I've just checked my account and they're still not there.

What's happening? This kind of thing has never been a problem in the eight or nine seasons I've played at the club. And the timing couldn't be worse: we're due to face the league leaders, Bohemians, in Cork tonight.

A win might put us in the psychological driving seat for the title-deciding run of games. I hope in writing this that I can park the issue for the day and worry about it again tomorrow, but it'll be difficult. Players are bound to be distracted when we meet up later. In any event a win would be terrific for all the players' positions.

circa 6pm, Turner's Cross

In the dressing room before the match the Gaffer tells us he's had his sources check whether the money has gone through, and it has.

"Your wages will definitely be accessible by you on Monday, lads."

League of Ireland Premier Division: Turner's Cross, Cork

Cork City 0–1 Bohemians

We dominate the first half but fail to score. Their striker, Glen Crowe, scores with an opportunistic effort in the second half and we're beaten. After the match Mathews comes into the dressing room and starts shouting at myself and goalkeeper Mick Devine about the goal. Certainly I was partially responsible as I lost a header in the lead-up, but those marking Crowe are not mentioned and that annoys me.

Monday 11th August

I've been annoyed over the weekend about their goal and the result, but today at least the wages have finally gone into our accounts, as promised by Mathews.

Wednesday 13th August

We were due to be paid again on Friday but we we've been paid today instead, two days early. Captain Dan Murray (Muzza) explains it best when he says, "Now something is definitely up."

Thursday 14th August

As I drive to training at Bishopstown (which we still use even though the club doesn't own the ground anymore) I'm already looking forward to tomorrow's FAI Cup clash in Dublin against Shamrock Rovers. We all want to put last week's defeat behind us. Rovers have been steadily improving under their young manager Pat Scully – to the point where they're beginning to forget that they went into examinership a few years ago – but we're the Cup holders and determined to keep it. A big crowd is expected and I can't wait.

But then the radio announces, "Cork City FC is looking to go into examinership, with reported debts of up to €800,000."

I park my car and walk into the dressing room. As usual, Mick Devine, the club's number one goalkeeper for the past eight or nine years, is also early. He's sitting alone on the uncomfortable, two-plank, low wooden benches that seem to encircle most dressing rooms. I tell him the news.

"For f***'s sake," he says, dropping his newspaper. He stares up at me blankly.

Cillian Lordan arrives in next (Cillian, like me but unlike most of the other lads in our squad, has completed his secondary and college education – in the form of an accountancy degree – and thus at least has something to fall back on should the club go bust) and the three of us discuss the news sombrely. We're all a bit shocked.

The other players flow in and most have already heard, but nobody really knows what the examinership process entails. The general consensus is that we should wait and see what the Gaffer says. The only person who doesn't show any uncertainty is long-suffering club secretary and legend of the club, Jerry Harris. Grey-haired Jerry has been here before with other Cork clubs (such as Cork Alberts in the 1980s); he's unmistakably gloomy, which is not like him.

Training begins and ends at a low tempo. Everyone seems distracted. Afterwards Mathews doesn't say much – only that it's bad news but we'll know more over the next few days, and that he'll keep us posted as soon as he hears anything. On the way out I meet him in the car park as he's parked next to me. He says he feels all our work has been undermined, and that "players will leave and we'll be brought apart."

Article entitled 'Who are the owners of Cork City?' – published in the *Irish Independent* on Friday 15th August 2008:

THEY are arguably the most marketable club in the League of Ireland with good attendances, a decent stadium and a large catchment area with no opposition of substance. Yet the tragic reality is that this morning, Cork City's very survival hangs in the balance. While the last couple of years on Leeside have featured a fair share of peaks and troughs, few imagined that it would come to this.

What is lacking is certainty, both in terms of the future and the exact method by which the League of Ireland title contenders have arrived at this situation. Their creditors know what they are owed, and it has been speculated that Cork could be as much as €800,000 in debt. Clarifying who will pick up that tab as well as keep the club in existence is another matter altogether. With scenarios like entering receivership or examinership being floated, the 3,500 punters who venture to Turner's Cross on a regular basis have a mountain of questions that need answering.

Who are the owners of Cork City?

The Arkaga fund are widely recognised as the owners of Cork City, with Brian Lennox selling the club to them last year. However, it has been suggested that there are complications with the transfer of ownership but despite that it is Arkaga who have been paying the wages and appointing people to call the shots.

Who are Arkaga?

Arkaga, founded by Irishman Gerard Walsh, are a private equity fund that invest principally in the healthcare, technology, property, media and leisure sectors. They are also engaged in stocks and real estate. They have offices in Jersey, London and Dublin.

So, who is owed money?

The list of Cork's creditors include the Munster FA, from whom they rent Turner's Cross, kit suppliers Hummel, local club Mayfield United and food providers, amongst others. Player payments are up to date, but they recently went three weeks without wages. Yesterday's panic arose amid the suggestion that Arkaga were now looking to pull the plug on further investment. The option of High Court examinership is being strongly considered, although Cork reacted angrily to reports yesterday that it was the course of action which had been decided upon.

Shamrock Rovers went through this process three years ago and were deducted league points while an agreement was reached whereby creditors were repaid with the Revenue Commissioners receiving seven cent in the euro and others 3.5 cent in the euro. Rovers were relegated but quickly bounced back and are now a solid part-time entity.

But why would Arkaga not be liable for the club's debts?

This is where things get confusing. There's no question that it has been involved in Cork's business, dealing with the FAI, drawing down the money to pay players, and recently meeting Mathews for talks about the club's future. However, its liability is unclear, and again this comes back to the technicalities surrounding the transfer of ownership and the very classification of Arkaga itself.

The FAI yesterday released a statement saying they had contacted the Arkaga Fund with regards to a written undertaking made by one of its companies to guarantee all liabilities arising from Cork City Investment FC Ltd for a 12-month period from January 29, 2008 through to January 29, 2009. Nobody, from either Cork or the FAI, was willing to reveal the name of this company – thought to be a parent of Cork City Investment FC Ltd – when contacted by the Irish Independent yesterday.

Where have the FAI been through all of this?

The FAI will argue that they will not discourage investment in any League of Ireland club, and plenty of people in Cork viewed Arkaga as a welcome arrival with financial clout. Their statement yesterday said:

"It is the FAI's view that the club's sustainability depends on its investors and directors managing the company's affairs as a sensible business.

"We await news of what the Arkaga Fund, as investors in Cork City Investment FC Ltd, intend to do.

"If Cork City Investment FC Ltd is in financial difficulty, then the onus is on the club's investors and directors to take all necessary corrective action to ensure its survival.

"The FAI has been and will continue to provide professional assistance to assist the club in any way possible at this difficult time."

Nevertheless, the overall scenario adds fuel to the flames of recent crises around the league, with a number of senior figures involved in the game calling for strong leadership from the top. Considering they receive monthly accounts from each club, they will have been aware of mounting debts on Leeside.

Certainly, the healthy prognosis offered by John Delaney at the recent FAI AGM rings hollow, with the CEO stating that "the hard work of the clubs and the new league team is clearly working."

One club who wished to raise the financial problems being felt around the country were advised against doing so because the press were present. This culture of denial has not helped the FAI's cause, particularly now, when one of their leading clubs is in dire straits.

What is the mood in the dressing room?

Mathews, who quit a lucrative banking job to commit himself to Cork full time, could not hide his disappointment yesterday. "I'm thinking about my future, my family's future, the players and their families' future," he said. "This is our livelihood. People have committed an awful lot and I hope that the people who are administering this football club will ensure that the best efforts are made to keep people in employment."

Naturally, the players are concerned. Joe Gamble, whose girlfriend gave birth to their first child earlier this week, turned down a monster contract with St Patrick's Athletic to sign a new contract with Cork last month. Understandably, he is wondering what he has got himself in for.

The entire debacle has overshadowed preparations for a huge FAI Ford Cup clash with Shamrock Rovers at Tolka Park tonight. In the context of their current plight, the best result for Cork would be a draw and a replay in front of a bumper crowd at Turner's Cross, where the fans have remained loyal throughout the turmoil.

Are we heading for another Shelbourne situation?
While the demise of Shels was somewhat different, they were ultimately demoted due to financial problems and suffered a mass exodus. It remains to be

seen what sanctions Cork could face. If a rescue package can be found to get them through this season, or Arkaga commit to providing cash until January and then pull out, then they may escape the drop but, either way, a return to part time football is likely.

Nine players are out of contract in November, with key figures like Colin Healy, Liam Kearney, John O'Flynn and Neal Horgan amongst them. They will have offers from elsewhere. Meanwhile, if Gamble or other contracted stars like Dave Mooney go without their wages for a few weeks, then they would be entitled to apply for free agent status, the method by which most players secured their release from Shels.

Why did Arkaga invest in Cork?

The motivation for Arkaga investing in Cork has never been established. They are strong supporters of the proposed All Ireland League – in fact early meetings regarding its establishment took place in their Dublin office – and are thought to be frustrated about the obstacles that stand in its way, with the FAI and IFA

unwilling to buy into the idea in the structure put
forward by Platinum One.

So, what happens next?

Cork say they have engaged in negotiations with
"potential new investors" for the last few weeks, and
some members of the business community in the south
have come out publicly to state their interest. In
reality, though, the situation with the mounting debts
needs to be addressed first. In a brief statement
yesterday, Cork said their board will meet next week
and "come to a decision on the future of the club." The
suspicion, however, is that their fate is ultimately out
of their hands.

~

Friday 15th August

The team bus stops at a hotel on the outskirts of
Dublin for food and a team meeting. Mathews starts
talking about the recent club difficulties. He says the

only thing we can do is try and control the football side of things – everything else is out of our hands.

But it doesn't take long to see the effect the recent news is having on the lads. In the first ten minutes we're all over the place, everyone making uncharacteristic mistakes. Our bodies are here but our minds are not. After a brief tongue-lashing by Mathews during the break we improve, and late on Denis Behan scores. We hold on. Everyone's happy – for a while.

F.A.I Cup (third round): Tolka Park, Dublin
Shamrock Rovers 0–1 Cork City

Monday 18th August

Our training ground in Bishopstown includes a fairly makeshift gym; it's located in the largest of the numerous rooms deep inside the lonely, defunct stand. In parts of the room you have to duck to avoid the diagonal rows of seating that rise overhead.

This morning our fitness coach, Cathal, has just enough free weights and space to put us through a fairly intense weights circuit, and after that we toil through a tough session out on the pitch. We have a few days off coming up so the Gaffer works us hard.

In the showers afterwards the lads talk about the fact that Dave Mooney, our striker, might be moving to Reading. Obviously the club could do with the money, but he'll be a big loss. 'Moons' is unusually quiet about the whole thing.

Wednesday 20th August

The Gaffer stands in the middle of the dressing room, surrounded by about 20 professional footballers. Each player is quiet and focused on every word that's coming out of his mouth. The scene is reminiscent of a young general about tell his squadron that war has broken out.

Mathews clears his throat before beginning.

"As you all know, the club has gone into examinership. What this actually means, lads, is that there might be a chance of survival. Most of you also know that Moons has gone to Reading for something like €250,000, so while it's sad to see him go and we wish him the best, at least that money will help. Now, in effect, Cork City Football Club has something like 100 days to get its act together and pay its bills to the Revenue."

Nobody stirs. The Gaffer takes a breath before continuing, "But it doesn't make any sense to me. How could Arkaga put so much money in and then just walk away? Some of you might remember seeing Gerard Walsh out here at the training ground a few months ago, but he didn't stay around to chat. Well, I've asked him to come back next Tuesday and explain what's happening. I'm not sure he'll turn up, although he said he would."

Front gunman Denis Behan is first to offer his thoughts: "He will in his f*** turn up Gaffer. No chance. And what's the story with the money for Mooney?"

The Gaffer explains that it can't be paid in advance but that we, as employees, will be at the head of the creditors to get paid. He then checks himself and says, "and maybe it'll all be there and maybe it won't."

"But what do you think, Gaffer, will it be there or not?" asks super-keeper Mick Devine, with customary defiance.

"I don't honestly know, Mick."

Mick, unhappy with this response, storms out of the room and into the toilets without another word.

Joe Gamble then breaks in like a little Spitfire: "How in the hell could the club have got into so much debt, Gaffer?"

Mathews attempts to wave off this attack by telling us the amounts of money involved, but he's interrupted by Mick, who returns to the gathering and bluntly declares, "I think we're all f***ed anyway," before throwing himself down across a masseur's bench in the middle of the room.

Mathews pauses for a moment as if he's about to say something to Mick, but then continues to explain the financial side of things to the rest of us. I, for one, don't really take it in; I look at Mick who has his head in his hands (goalkeeper's gloves on) and is lying face-down on the masseur's bench in the middle of the scene.

Gamble, however, is listening. "Look, lads. We're all in this together. There's a good group of lads here – we just need to stick together and we'll be alright."

Captain Dan Murray (Muzza) adds, "Ya lads – like Gamble says, stick together and we'll be stronger. All we can do is wait and see what happens."

The Gaffer, in an attempt to end on a high note, adds, "Well anyway, there's always the possibility of money coming into the club from the sell-on clause that we have if Kevin Doyle's moving on from Reading, and there are rumours that he might – although that's obviously not something to rely on at the moment."

The meeting finishes and we go out and train, but despite the Gaffer's best efforts heads are down and the lads are quiet.

A few hours later I'm at home and Muzza rings, asking could I come with him and Gamble[1] to meet up with the newly appointed examiner in the club shop. I agree, keen to find out for myself what's going on.

Daunt Square, Cork

Alan Mathews accompanies the three of us to the top of the club shop. To my surprise the examiner turns out to be a guy of about 35, rather than the unapproachable high-browed elderly type that, I suspect, we had all imagined. He welcomes us briefly before getting down to business, starting with the good news:

---

[1] Joe, Muzza and myself had previously been involved in discussions with Arkaga regarding the matter of unpaid bonuses for winning the FAI Cup. We were semi-successful then, so Muzza decided to go with the same trio again.

1. There are people interested in taking over the club already.

2. The initial sum for Mooney is very promising at such an early stage of examinership.

3. CCFC is a big club with a lot of fans, and from his experience of going through examinership with Shamrock Rovers, nobody wants to lose a good customer.

4. There is still a lot of goodwill attached to the club.

The examiner then looks at me square in the eyes and soberly states, "However, there will be hard times ahead – have no doubt about it."

I gulp. He must be planning to get rid of me.

Muzza and Gamble ask about the players' futures, and before the examiner can reply the Gaffer explains to him how some players have long contracts but others' are up in November (at end of this season). Then the Gaffer, looking directly at Gamble and Muzza, suggests that he himself would be capable of trimming the squad if necessary. I try desperately to catch his eye to make sure I'm part of his plans, but without joy.

The examiner, oblivious to my paranoia, changes the subject in haste: "So what this all means is that there are various creditors, including the Revenue, who will be kept at bay until the examinership process is concluded. In the meantime," he says, "the gate receipts of any match will be used for match-day expenses and the rest will be used to pay the players. How much is there for the players' wages will therefore obviously depend on how many fans turn up to watch you play."

Muzza suggests getting the players to use their connections in the local media to ask the fans to come out and support the club. The examiner assents to this and tells us he'll know more in the next few weeks. He agrees to meet us the following week to update us on events. He also asks us to lay off Gerard Walsh, as in his experience of high-end, executive, wealthy investors, if they feel unappreciated they'll just leave.

"So if you do get to meet him, my advice would be to ask him to live up to his end of things, but don't abuse him."

"If he turns up, that is," adds Muzza.

While cordially steering us out, perhaps in an effort to comfort us, the examiner says that overall he would be optimistic regarding a takeover of some sort.

Thursday 21st August

The rest of the lads are anxious to know how we got on with the examiner and the three of us fill them in: the Mooney money is a good thing... we need to lay off Gerard Walsh if he comes in... there are others interested in taking over... he'll speak with us again during the week. This seems to satisfy most of them, but I notice little Liam Kearney holding his tongue, fire in his eyes. Thankfully it's time for training and I rush out.

In training we do quite a lot: warm-up, passing drills, fast feet, game of transfer, 8 v 8 game. On the pitch after training Mathews calls us together and talks about tomorrow's opponents, Bray Wanderers. He goes through what he believes to be their strengths and weaknesses; he reminds us to remain focused on the job.

The goalkeeping coach, 'Biscuits' (Phil Harrington), who had been hovering nearby, bursts in: "Yeez bloody need the three points, lads. Yeez need to focus on that. That's all yeez can be thinking about."

As we're walking in, left-back Darragh Ryan approaches me with obvious caution, looking around us to see who's nearby. He whispers, "I've come up with an idea to make some money over Christmas if the club goes under and we're unemployed: we'll set up a Santa's Grotto with Kearney, Murph and Gamble [a trio of short, angry players] as Santa's little elves. We'll make a fortune, bud!"

Friday 22nd August

Before the start of the match, as is normal procedure, we gather in a huddle, arm-in-arm. Muzza's up with the referees and the Bray captain in the middle of the pitch. We all wait to see who wins the toss.

"Stay as we are!" shouts Muz. He's lost the toss again. "I never win that f***ing thing," he murmurs, running back to join the huddle.

Just before Muzza starts his pep talk, Healers (Colin Healy) turns to look at the crowd over his shoulder and says, laughingly, "I'm not sure there's enough fans here to pay our wages, lads."

Crazy Daz and others also turn, seriously attempting an estimate, before Muzza hauls them back with his English-accent curses. "We're here to win the match, f*** everything else!"

We play well. Gamble gets a goal and then Denis Behan gets two. The crowd weighs in at 3,795.

During the match the fans sing, *"They don't care about Mathews, they don't care about fans, CCFC is in the wrong hands, its in the wrong haaaaands... Cork City Football Club is in the wrong hands."*

They sing it over and over, to the point where it gets irritating (to me, at least). But their devotion to the club comes across clearly.

League of Ireland: Turner's Cross, Cork
Cork City 3–0 Bray Wanderers

The fans sing until well after the match is over, and then all through the warm-down. There's still about 800 of them left even half an hour after that. Lordy and I discuss this on the way to the dressing room, agreeing that five or ten years ago there would've been about 80 of them hanging about – and most of them would've just been waiting to throw abuse. Without the fans' current support, would there be hope for the club? No, there wouldn't. They've saved Cork City FC from obscurity by turning up in great numbers and backing the club in times of need – and in doing so they've become a greater part of it than ever before. Isn't this what a club's all about? The fans seem to be stepping up to the mark and showing their support more readily than ever; maybe these difficult times will be the making of this club for generations to come. Maybe I should be thanking Arkaga for unintentionally setting the scene for a resurgence...

On leaving tonight I say Hi to all the usual fans that are hanging around the ground. On approaching my car I hear "Hoggie!" (my nickname) called out. It's Ian Sheehan – a hardcore member of the CCFC supporters who organises fans' buses (of the drinking variety) to away games. He asks about the club situation and about the players. I tell him I think, sadly, that the cream of players will leave – the top-earning full-timers.

Later, thinking about it, I realise what's at stake is not just the survival of CCFC but also that of full-time football in Cork – and progress in the Irish domestic game. The progress we've made over the last few years could count for nothing. To make any serious headway in the lucrative European competitions, full-time football is a prerequisite.

Saturday 23rd August

Our recovery day is normally spent in a local hotel swimming pool, but today it's been cancelled. Players aren't sure why, although some say it just wasn't organised. Later we find out the hotel shut the door on us because we owed them money.

Monday 25th August

We're one down at home against Wexford Youths. Deep into the second half, the crowd's on our backs. Their keeper's having the game of his life while all the lads – including me – have missed good chances to score. Denis in particular is having no luck.

Winger Liam Kearney, like the rest of us, isn't having a great day, and he's getting flak from somewhere behind him in the crowd. Kearney gets the ball, tries to play a cross-field pass, miscues, and the ball ends up in their keeper's hands. Same fella shouts at Kearney again, and this time Kearney reacts: he turns and puts two fingers up and, unable to decipher exactly who the perpetrator is, tells the whole area of the crowd to go f*** themselves. Unfortunately he's just vented his frustration at the family enclosure. But Kearney is unmoved and plays on without any apparent regret.

They hold on and we walk off, heads down under the pressure of the boos (from the Shed End in particular). As we're walking into the tunnel a CCFC 'fan' hangs over the barrier, waving and shouting at Denis, who's next to me.

"Denis you f***ing useless pr*ck... You're some pr*ck, Behan!"

Thankfully Denis, whose skin is thicker than mine, doesn't respond.

League Cup semi-final: Turner's Cross, Cork
Cork City 0–1 Wexford Youths

In the dressing room the Gaffer has a go at us, but he's more restrained than he usually is when we lose. We sit in silence for a while.

Then more bad news: Gerard Walsh won't be meeting us tomorrow after all. It's disappointing and frustrating for everyone. Mathews later points out that we're due to meet the examiner tomorrow morning for an update on possible investors and our positions at the club.

Later I find it hard to sleep. Although it's only the League Cup, the fact that we've been beaten by a team from the first division is embarrassing and damaging. We're in the early stages of examinership, attempting to prove that full-time football is a viable prospect in Cork, and we lose to a predominantly amateur side. The possibility that the final might have been played in Cork, guaranteeing a much-needed earner (possibly €60,000 with a full house) against Derry City, makes this a really dark day.

Tuesday 26th August

Discussion of Kearney's display of rage, and a few other stories, keep myself and Darragh Ryan entertained in the pool (which the hotel have allowed us back into) despite the general feeling of depression.

Fitness coach Cathal, who spoke to the Gaffer on the phone this morning, tells us, "You should hear him – he's the most depressed man on the planet."

We all know there'll be no joy, or even relief, until we win another game. We really could have done with Dave Mooney last night. Damn it anyway; it's important just to move on now and forget about it.

Wednesday 27th August

More bad news today. Before we arrived at training, Jerry Kelly, our quirky groundsman, had phoned the club office, concerned about the positions of his colleagues in the club shop. During the call he's told that the players are to receive only 30% of their wages.

Jerry, pitchfork in hand, informs goalkeeper Mark McNulty, who wastes no time in announcing it to the rest of the lads in the dressing room.

Everyone's trying to work out 30% of their own fortnightly wage; most do these calculations silently, but Denis, upsettingly for everyone else, is doing his out loud. The results cause panic among the lads.

"Maybe it's not true," one says.

"Who said it was true anyway?" says another.

"Wait and see what they say."

"What *who* says? Who's coming to see us?"

"The examiner fella and Pat Kenny – the fella running the club the last few weeks. Let's finally ask our questions, and get our answers."

"And no f***ing messing and joking like the in the last meetings," orders Colin Healy.

Denis Behan responds to this by nodding his head up and down like a puppy dog – the same Denis who usually interrupts the most serious of meetings with terrible and often indecipherable jokes.

The Gaffer then enters the dressing room. He says he had problems getting in touch with the examiner but that he's now due to meet him, with the same three players, after training. Kearney says he'd prefer all the players to be there; I heartily agree, knowing how difficult it would be to explain a complicated situation to an angry group of professional footballers – and to Kearney in particular.

"OK Liamo – I've no problem with that. And just so you lads know, there's still no sign of Gerard Walsh," says Mathews.

He then says he's been told by the examiner there's not enough money to cover the wages and we're going to be offered a reduced wage. He's not sure how much. He says the examiner has been laying off members of the club office staff, and if it comes down to it "he'll have to lay people off out here too."

Gamble suggests, "Fellas might have to go on loan, Gaffer."

"I've no problem with that. I'll support yee," Mathews replies.

He then tries to talk about last Monday. "But f***ing hell, boys – 33 shots; 16 on target; a missed penalty…" he turns to Crazy Daz (Darren Murphy), "and one example that summed up the night. I'm not blaming you, Daz, but that shot near the end – it looked like you had your boots tied together, the way you hit it!"

I don't hear Daz's response (although I'm sure it was some novel excuse or other) but all the lads have a laugh.

Then Mathews interjects in a serious tone: "Anyway lads, the fact is we've got to get our heads back on the game for Friday."

We go out and train but the mood is very low.

Afterwards Mathews tells us to hurry up and get showered and changed as the examiner has come to see us, along with Pat Kenny. The lads oblige and there is, perhaps naively, a sense of nervous excitement among the group that we're finally getting to meet with the examiner. Players rush into the large meeting room around the corner from our dressing rooms, and before long all the seats are taken. The stragglers, including me, have to stand at the back or sit uncomfortably at the edge of tables.

Players' meeting with examiner

The examiner is seated at the top of the room. He sits facing the players, while Pat Kenny – CEO for the last few months – sits at a desk slightly behind him to the left. Mathews takes a seat at a desk to the examiner's right. Super-keeper Mick Devine, true to form, has chosen to sit up between the Gaffer and Pat Kenny, directly behind the examiner.

After a brief introduction the examiner explains, "Basically there's not enough money to cover the wages of staff and players." He says the club currently has enough for about 30% of players' wages, taken from the gates of the last two games.

"However, since we [himself and Kenny] have laid off four office staff today, this percentage could increase. He says this in a respectful tone, and pauses briefly before continuing to explain that he's looking at all aspects of the club, including the roles of playing staff and of the players themselves.

Pat Kenny, looking grim behind him, adds, "It really hasn't been a good day."

The audience takes an aggressive line of questioning. Mick, from behind the examiner, asks, "*You* get paid though, don't ya?"

The examiner turns to face Mick and replies that he does. He then proceeds to answers further questions from the players in a factual and efficient manner.

He raises the possibility of a higher wage if other players, outside of those present, are left out altogether. This would mean non-payment for players currently out on loan or out sick (including Gareth Farrelly) or injured, or those not needed in the Gaffer's or examiner's opinion.

He explains, "That would bring wages up to 38%, or something like it. But I want to know how you, the players and playing staff, feel about it before we decide anything. So what do you think?"

Gamble responds first, "I don't think we can cut those boys off, to be honest. We've got to stick together." This is backed by a murmur of approval from the rest of the lads.

The Examiner reiterates, "Well, it'll be up to me – but I wanted to know how you feel about it first."

Gamble stands firm. "We couldn't approve the cutting of players as we're players ourselves – it wouldn't be right."

Again the lads agree: "You have to pay them, we have to stick together."

Denis speaks up: "Poor old John Tierney [a young player out on loan at Limerick], left with nothing. We can't be doing that."

Healy adds, "We can't stop paying Colin T, Woodsy and the boys."

Mick agrees: "Ya, you have to pay the boys," to which Lordy also declares his agreement.

Kearney stands up, clears his throat and says, "I think the general feeling from the players is that if you're going to pay any of us then you have to pay us all. It's unfair otherwise."

Pat Kenny and the examiner look at each other and I get the feeling they're impressed. Although it's only an 8% difference I still feel proud of the lads.

The Gaffer asks the examiner whether it would affect their position with the FAI if everyone was paid.

"Yes, it would look more favourable for the club if everyone's paid," he answers.

Cathal, the fitness coach, asks the examiner, "Are there other clubs in the league in this position, do you know?"

"I'd say some of them are, yes."

"So how come they're not in examinership?"

"Well, firstly, their wages aren't as high as they are here…"

Muzza explodes, shouting directly at the examiner, "You're taking the f***ing piss now if your saying Drogheda and Pat's are on less money than us!"

Luckily for the examiner the Gaffer intervenes. He (the Gaffer) thinks Bohemians have a slightly larger playing budget, with Drogheda's and St. Patrick's being significantly larger, and Derry's being similar to ours or slightly less.

The examiner lets the point go and, moving on, reveals that there are parties interested in taking over the club.

I ask him who would be deciding which investor takes the club.

"I'll decide," he says.

"So what would be the criteria for deciding between them?" I continue, "How much money they're offering, or...?"

"No. I'll be looking for the best investors for the survival and continuation of CCFC."

The players ask whether he can tell us who's interested; he says he can't do that yet, but he tells us there are two parties and both of them are genuinely interested – and willing to pay enough to bring players' wages up to 105% after gate receipts.

Muzza asks, politely, "Am I right in thinking players could move, in a few weeks, if they don't take the 30% and if a club's interested in them, as their contracts have been breached?"

"Yes, that's correct."

"Would it help the club, then, if these players were to go?"

"I'd prefer players to stay at the club, but if they do leave, then yes – the wage bill would obviously decrease and there would be more in the pot for the remaining players."

Mathews then confirms that if an investor does come in, "I'll honour any commitments I've already made to players that are out of contract at the end of the season."

Mick asks the examiner, "What if the club went back to part-time – would you see that as an option?"

Some of the players give out to Mick for asking. The examiner interrupts them to explain that while he hasn't ruled anything out as of yet, "the intention at the moment is to stay full time."

Mick retorts to the lads, half-apologetically, "I'm just asking..."

Then Gamble starts up: "Sorry, now, but I want to ask – where did all the f***ing money go?"

It's Pat Kenny that tries to explain: "Arkaga say they put in €2.4 million already. Into players' wages, staff wages, redeveloping Bishopstown and all the other things they've done." And with a very serious demeanour he adds, "They are unequivocal now; they are spending no more money and cutting all ties with the club."

This angers me, but Denis does my talking: "So they got us into this and just walked away, and now we're the ones that are suffering?"

Full-back Danny Murphy adds, "How could they not budget? Why offer so much money to the players if they didn't have it?"

Gamble contributes, "Players wouldn't be looking for money if the club didn't have it. Just don't sign the players if the money's not there – then they could go elsewhere."

Mathews partially answers, "They probably do have the money, Joe, but it's tied up elsewhere. We're dealing with successful and ruthless businessmen here; they've decided to walk away and they know how to do it."

At this point Mick gets up, huffing and puffing, excuses himself and walks through everyone on his way out.

Muzza brings up the question of the FAI guarantee, but I'm distracted by Mick pinching my leg on the way out and I only hear something about jurisdictional difficulties, and that it looks like the FAI are not going to pursue it.

The examiner finishes up by asking us to remain positive in the media.

"If you can remain as positive as possible it might help the chances of a takeover."

Mathews thanks him for coming in, as do the players. Some wait to ask him questions privately – Denis first among them.

~

Players' meeting with the Gaffer

Players flow down the corridor and back into the dressing room, where the Gaffer eventually calls us together and tells us he'll remain at the club unpaid, if necessary, until the end of the season. He asks us to let him know if we can't make training.

Gamble suggests training at night for those who need to get another job.

The Gaffer answers, "Let's wait and see, Joe. The best thing at this stage is probably to take things on a week-by-week basis, and if the need for change arises, we'll do so."

Murph adds, despairingly, "No f***ing way am I training at night. I've got to train full time to get a move or I'll get fat as a fool."

"You mean fatter than you already are?" Kearney jibes with typical speed.

Finally Mathews explains that the fans' group FORAS has set up a meeting for tonight, and it might be a good thing if we attend to show our support. Most of the lads agree to go along.

~

FORAS meeting: Telecom Club, MacCurtain Street, Cork, 8pm

The lads arrive in twos and threes and hang about by the Metropole Hotel, a comfortable 100 yards from the fans who are congregating by the meeting room. While we're waiting for people to turn up, Lordy tells us that Denis is off to Norway.

"At least they might be able to understand him there," quips Mick.

"He's flown over already," someone else says – at which point Denis himself comes strolling around the corner.

He's cross-examined.

"It's not out of the question," he says. "My agent's onto me about it alright."

Denis has heard that the assistant manager, Paul 'Skee' McGee, and our fitness coach Cathal are gone from the club as well. Gamble adds that he heard from

120

the PFAI (the players' union in Ireland) that we might be relegated and banned from Europe for three years.

The lads are struggling to take it all in. Murph whispers to me, "I don't know about you, mate, but I can't take any more bad news."

Deputy goalkeeper Mark McNulty then spots Brian Lennox walking past the fans into the meeting room, and says to me, amazed, "He'll get lynched Hogs – he's some balls to be fair to him!"

"He probably just wants to give his side," I reply. I'm reminding myself of why we're going to this meeting: to support the fans' initiative. We'll wait until they go in and then we'll follow.

In the meantime notorious local scribe Noel Spillane ('Spillachi'), radioman Billy Barry and photographer Eddie O'Hare arrive, circling the players like dolphins hunting fish. There's a flash, and then another as Eddie starts taking photos of us talking, as if we're models. Someone – probably Healers – shouts, "F*** off Eddie!" Eddie stops, but only briefly before continuing unopposed. Spillachi moves in on

Mick for an exclusive, while Muzza's grabbed by Billy Barry.

We notice that the fans have gone in so now it's our turn. "Wrap it up," someone says, and we move. On the way Spillachi sneaks over to me and asks for a "short piece." I agree, and he shoves his 1970s vintage dictaphone a few inches from my face as we walk down MacCurtain street. Eddie then starts focussing on us… *flash, flash*. I'm desperately trying to remember what we agreed to say – and what we agreed not to say – to the media. I try to be positive: "...hopefully someone will save club..." but then, perhaps distracted by the lights, I mention something about losing the cream of our players over the next few weeks. I immediately realise I need to withdraw this, but it's too late. We're at the entrance and Spillachi breaks off.

Fans watch with bated breath us as we come in. It's an old fashioned room with weird, reddish bohemian carpets and wallpaper. As we walk in it feels particularly warm, even though the windows are wedged wide open.

It's mostly the hardcore supporters, many of whom I recognise, but there are others present that I don't know. Their expressions are anxious and there's a sense that things are falling apart.

It's very hard to hear people talking on the platform. The first speaker is a FORAS representative; he begins by explaining that FORAS are here to provide assistance to the club if at all possible. Half-way through his speech, some of the crowd at the back shout out that they can't hear what he's saying. A microphone is brought in, but it soon breaks down and the guy has to continue without it.

Club administrator Éanna Buckley then soberly informs the room about the layoff of certain administrative and playing staff. He finishes by introducing Brian Lennox.

I whisper to Brian as he passes me on his way up, "I'll jump on for you if things get ugly." He laughs and continues to the head of the room.

Brian speaks about the last few weeks, months and years. He's questioned vigorously by the audience and in my opinion comes out quite well.

Centre-forward John O'Flynn whispers to me, "He shouldn't have to do this."

I say, "Maybe he wants to face them and show he's not running away."

Brian gets a nice applause as he finishes up.

Alan Mathews speaks briefly, explaining the situation he and the players are in. He talks in a restrained manner – perhaps uncertain of how much to divulge – but on stepping down he's applauded nonetheless.

Dan Murray's next up.

"The first thing to say is that the players at the back of the room are probably taking bets on how much I'll curse, so I'll try not to for a change."

He speaks about the difficulties the players have had lately; how we wish we'd known earlier what was going on. "The interesting thing, if you think about it though, is that the club is going back to its heart – to the volunteers – to the way it was years ago when I first joined."

Throughout this our scribe Spillachi is stood at the back of the hall, his back to the stage, typing noisily away on a laptop. I sneak up and read my piece over his shoulder; it seems fine, thank God, so I go back to listening to Muzza.

"I also have to say that everything you've seen and heard up until now, in the papers or on the radio or whatever, is…" he pauses, struggling to find the right word. There's hushed silence. He clears his throat: "...everything you've heard is absolute b***ocks! I'd say the situation is a lot f***ing worse than anything you've f***ing heard."

He finishes by promising that the players "will do our best to win, no matter what," and he gets a standing ovation.

Impatient creatures that we players are, we begin to stir, pass off a collective goodbye and leave as a group. The meeting continues in our absence.

Thursday 28th August

Part-timer Woodsy is at training for the first time in ages, but the lads are quick to welcome him back, calling him a 'trialist' as he's grown his hair long. Kearney jokes, "We're down to 30% because of you, ya pr**k!"

Woodsy enjoys the banter.

During warm-up Crazy Daz asks, in jest, "Where's Cathal, Gaffer?" (Fitness coach Cathal O'Shea would usually take the warm-ups.) The Gaffer doesn't laugh.

We play a small-sided game, but players are in bad form and there are a few near-fisticuffs. Afterwards I chat to Kearney while we're sat cleaning our boots on the way in. He says he really doesn't want to leave Cork again.

Friday 29th August

We're away to Shamrock Rovers for a league game. On the bus to Dublin, brown envelopes enclosing our 30% wages are handed out. It's probably a bad move.

The lads are dejected enough already, given that last night on the radio we heard we're being deducted ten points in the league due to examinership. Seeing in physical form the 70% decrease in our wages just adds to the misery.

The lads are all talking about their futures; people discuss who can move and where to. Denis is still on the way to Norway, apparently. A load of scouts are supposed to be at the game tonight, including a couple from Club Brugge and Notts County.

At the hotel after pre-match the Gaffer holds a meeting. He says he's heard there's an interested investor who has a brownfield site and wants to develop the club on this. Muzza's not convinced, though: "It sounds like f***ing Arkaga all over again."

We get to Tolka Park and in the dressing room the Gaffer's on about bouncing back. Flynny (injured) and Murph (suspended) take the warm-up in place of assistant manager Skee McGee. It's all very amateurish. Players are trying hard to gee each other up and concentrate on winning the game, but to me, at least, it feels a little too forced.

Despite this we start well and dominate for a while before they score against the run of play. Then in the second half Gamble gets sent off and they get a second, then a third. We're all over the place. Pat Sullivan gets injured at the death and is stretchered off. It's live on national TV; I've never before known the team or the club to be so exposed.

League of Ireland: Tolka Park, Dublin
Shamrock Rovers 3–0 Cork City

There's a feeling of emptiness in the dressing room afterwards. On the bus on the way home the news is that Denis is definitely moving.

Saturday 30th August

The next day's headlines all agree: it's been the worst week in the history of the club. And it's hard to argue with that. This morning our recovery is in a different hotel, in the northside of the city. We're told the usual hotel is no longer available to us as they haven't been paid.

I haven't slept: bizarrely, I got a minor whiplash-type injury during the game last night (as I jumped to block a shot I was pushed in the back just as the ball hit me in the head) and my neck is very sore.

Sunday 31st August

I meet Denis in the car park before training. He explains that his agent told him his deal didn't go through as "the FAI don't work on Sundays." He seems really annoyed with this. "And Flynny has signed for Barnet," he adds, dejectedly.

Everyone's sorry to see Flynny leave. He and George O'Callaghan had returned home from England after the ITV 'digital deal' collapse in 2002/03; signed by Liam Murphy on the same day, the two of them had got on like a house on fire, happily causing mayhem in hotel rooms, buses, restaurants and team meetings. They were also virtually telepathic on the pitch, with skilful George adept at putting the speedy O'Flynn through on goal. On the good days they were simply electric. Without them it feels like a voltage charge has been removed from the team and from the city.

Lawrie Dudfield (a centre-forward recently signed from England) has gone back to England too, so there's a good few young players training, up from the under-21s. My neck's in bits, but as there's no physio at training (Alex is only coming in half the time now) there's nothing I can do but sit in the empty stand and watch.

Biscuits takes training as the Gaffer's been in Belfast watching Cliftonville – our opponents for tomorrow. After training we travel to Dundalk, where we'll stay overnight before moving onto Belfast. It feels like we've not left the bus since Friday.

Chapter Five

1st to 7th September 2008

Monday 1st September

This morning at our hotel in Dundalk I finally get treatment on my neck from our physio, Alex. I'm eager to update Mathews about it – to let him know it's still very painful – so I go down to the lobby area talk to him and on the way I meet Denis in the corridor. He's on his way to talk to the Gaffer about moving to another club. Wycombe and Notts County are in for him, he says. He meets the Gaffer first, and as he's taking ages I decide to go back to bed.

At 4.15pm we're down for pre-match pasta. The Gaffer pulls me aside and says, "Alex says you're struggling, so I'll leave you out, but we need to fill the numbers so would you go on the bench?"

"Ya, no bother, Gaffer," I say with relief.

"Sully [Pat Sullivan] is on it too, and he's just off crutches, but there's seven subs in this competition and I don't have anyone else. Thanks for doing it, anyway."

The Gaffer's pre-match speech is exhaustive of Cliftonville's abilities and what we need to do to beat them. As usual he's specified, on charts around the room, what set pieces we should use. Their set pieces are also drawn out from the game he'd watched last week, when they were beaten 2–1 by Glentoran. I can tell he's trying hard to keep things as normal as possible and I'm glad he isn't letting up yet.

I don't enjoy being on the bench. I don't know how people do it, listening to the remarks of the manager and other staff.

At half time, club administrator Éanna Buckley tells me that he heard Kevin Doyle might be moving. "A transfer tonight would solve all our problems," he says. "Fingers crossed."

Denis has scored two good goals, so maybe he'll get his move after all. On the bus home, as the lads are pestering him about it, he says he's hoping his agent will sort it this time.

The bus driver keeps slamming on the brakes and the lads give him an awful time.

"Can't you f***ing see?!" shouts Denis. I wouldn't normally support shouting at bus drivers, but as this is not helping my whiplash I encourage Denis to continue with his attacks.

I finally nod off but I'm woken at 3.40am by Danny Murphy and Gamble, who are screaming at each other over a game of cards under the bus's faint overhead lights. Everyone else seems cosily asleep, basking in the comfort of an away victory.

I wake at 12 the next day and check all the usual sources to find that Kevin Doyle hasn't moved yet.

Wednesday 3rd September

This morning as I drive in I see the Gaffer, on his own on the pitch in the lashing rain, putting out cones for the session.

I get treatment from Alex, who tells me he's coming in unpaid at the moment. Boys are chatting in the dressing room about the *Irish Examiner* showing how to save €30,000. "We'll have to look into that," someone says.

Numbers are low for training: only ten outfield players, plus two goalkeepers. About four others are there but injured and not training. That's sixteen players in total.

I'm relieved to complete the session without too much difficulty – apart from the rain, which just lashes and lashes.

PFAI meeting

After training Muzza reminds us of a meeting at 1pm with Stephen McGuinness of the PFAI. It's in a local hotel, and when the time comes most players turn up promptly – apart from Gamble, who's late as usual.

When Gamble finally arrives, McGuinness, who's accompanied by a representative from SIPTU (a collection of unions of which the PFAI is a member), attempts to tell us the situation as he sees it.

The main point is that the 70% wage-cut should instead be considered a wage *deferral*, and that the club is obliged to pay us this money back before they can successfully apply for a license to operate in the league next year. McGuinness say he himself wrote a letter to the examiner about this, and the examiner then showed it to the judge in the case hearing that preceded examinership.

The SIPTU representative points out that the strongest thing we have going for us at the moment is that we stand in the way of the club getting a licence for next year. Any potential investors are likely to try and divide us in order to agree individual settlements and save themselves money, so we need to stick together.

It strikes me that this is the first time I'll be positioned against my club. I'm a Cork City fan, but also one of the more experienced players in the squad. Until now these two roles have existed in relative harmony.

McGuinness says he's spoken to the examiner and they hope to get the wages up to 50% by the next payment, due to John O'Flynn leaving and the fact that they're not paying Gareth Farrelly – a decision that has been made among other cuts. He compares Farrelly's situation to that of another player a few years ago at Shamrock Rovers. That player got his money in the end.

He says he and the PFAI will work to get the money we're already owed from the investor when he comes in.

"An investor is unlikely to come in now as he would have to pay all the debts, but if he waits until the examinership process is nearly over it would be better for him. You're not going to win the league; you're in the cups alright but financially there's nothing major for an investor to gain from taking over right now."

McGuinness stresses the significance of the timing of Arkaga's decision to apply for examinership. He thinks it was perfectly timed from their point of view to keep the players (being the only assets of CCFC) from pursuing their careers elsewhere.

"Had they done it four weeks before the transfer window closed, all of your main players would have gone as free agents to other Irish clubs. But they've timed it so players had very little chance to move anywhere. Transfer windows were closed in Ireland when they got out; if a player had wanted to move it would've had to have been cross-channel – and also very hurried, as the English transfer window was soon to close."

I'm a little confused by this, but before I can ask for a clearer explanation a photographer unexpectedly moves up around the players and starts taking pictures. Nobody had heard him coming into the room.

Colin Healy is the first to object, and he does so angrily: "What's the story with him, Stephen?"

McGuinness says, "I don't mind. Do yous not want him here?"

The photographer tells us he's working for the *Evening Echo* (the local paper), and that he was told he could take a few photos.

Crazy Daz points out that the Gaffer doesn't want photos as it'll look like a crisis meeting. "He said it would paint a negative picture in the local media, and we're trying to avoid that."

McGuinness: "Does anyone in particular object?"

Nobody says anything, apart from Crazy Daz who is still murmuring about the Gaffer.

McGuiness again says, "I don't care – let him take his photos."

Sully quips to the photographer, "Could you focus on Colin Healy?" and everyone laughs.

The photographer clicks away. I goad Crazy Daz: "The Gaffer's gonna go mad – he'll drop you over those pics."

He laughs and pokes me in the neck – which he knows is still sore – so I stop and turn back to McGuinness.

"In truth I believe yee could get deducted more than a mere ten points, and that relegation is still a distinct possibility – at least that's what I'm hearing up in the corridors in my place." (The PFAI are located in the same building in Abbotstown, Dublin as the FAI.)

Players, unsurprisingly, are not happy about this. Denis Behan fumes: "So we're being punished for Arkaga f***ing up."

McGuinness agrees, but he says he also thinks CCFC will have to be dealt with more sternly to stop them from going into examinership with a ten-point penalty in order to lose their creditors. Towering over us, he points out, "Sure, what's to stop Galway from doing it, for example? They're at the bottom of the league, struggling to stay up... ten points mightn't matter to them at the end of the day. Sure, why don't they just cut their losses like CCFC?"

He says he thinks CCFC should suffer, as they haven't been playing by the rules like everyone else. "There was a similar situation at Shelbourne a few years ago when they were signing everyone," he says, adding that he believes CCFC should be banned from Europe for three years as they haven't been able to pay their creditors in full. "The only way it would have been possible [to pay creditors in full] was if Kevin Doyle had been sold – and that's not going to happen now."

I look out the window. It's still raining.

McGuinness finishes by telling us he'll only be acting for players that are members of the PFAI, and that other players will have to chase the club for the money themselves. He'll need to be updated every week on what we're owed.

Afterwards the general consensus is to stick together so we can get as much of our wages back as possible and, more to the point, because we have no other choice. Apparently the Rovers players got 65% of what they were owed in the end.

Thursday 4th September

It's a glorious morning and the boys are in good form, probably due to the win in Belfast on Monday. As we come out, the Gaffer, standing by cones in the far corner of the pitch, beckons us. We stumble across as a group and he points out that only two players were out on pitch at 10.30am.

"There's no excuses, lads. If you need treatment, come in early. We can't let our standards drop. Alright?"

Lads mutter agreement. I appreciate his efforts to keep things working as planned. I also appreciate the brevity of his lecture; there's nothing worse for players' morale than standing around being lectured for ages, in the freezing cold, before the start of training. It can put a downer on the whole session.

Training commences and we go about our stuff in good form. Warm-up jog, then ball-work, passing warm-up (triangles and squares, following the ball), then small-sided games with two goalies, then team line-up. Working on defensive shape and then offensive play. From this we can almost be certain what the team line-up for tomorrow will be.

Friday 5th September

I wake up to find that my back garden has been flooded by near-torrential rain during the night. Later, while cooking pre-match dinner, I get a group text from the Gaffer: *Game off tonight. Back in on Monday morning, usual time.*

League of Ireland: Cork City vs Derry City
(called off due to water-logged pitch)

I'm elated as I need a break, so I ring Darragh Ryan to share the joy. He says he was actually looking forward to the game, and that Kearney, his flatmate, is pissed off because now we won't get paid.

I'd forgotten about that.

I'm starting to make plans for the weekend when I get another text from the Gaffer: *League forcing us to play Derry game on Monday, so in usual time for training Saturday and Sunday morning.*

At least we might get paid, I suppose. And however inconvenient the rearranged fixture is for me, imagine the inconvenience and cost for Derry. They came down last night and the match was called off today, so they'll come back down on Sunday for the game on Monday and then they're coming here again next weekend to play us in the FAI Cup… a 1,000km return trip by bus.

Later on, someone shows me an article in *The Phoenix* linking the pull-out of Arkaga to the failed plan for an All-Ireland league involving teams from both the Republic and Northern Ireland.

from *The Phoenix*, 5th September 2008:

Drury stated in an RTE interview last month that his plan for an All-Ireland league was conceived by him at a meeting of domestic soccer's heavyweights in Arkaga's offices in September 2007 [...] The plan stalled when (John) Delaney refused to back it. Shortly after the Irish Times reported that Denis O'Sullivan has apparently told a meeting of interested clubs that if the All-Ireland league did not come shortly to fruition Arkaga would have to bail out. Within a month of the IT report that is exactly what happened.

Saturday 6th September

It's raining heavily and the Gaffer throws a sneaky few runs at us midway through the training session. Gamble checks his heart-rate monitor after the second run and complains when the Gaffer shortens the recovery time before the third run.

   "Can't fool you, Joe!" the Gaffer says.

Gamble is ridiculously attentive to drills and training; I, on the other hand, am not.

Later I watch Ireland play on the TV. Kevin Doyle scores. Fair play to him.

Sunday 7th September

The Gaffer calls a meeting before training.

"Another f***ing meeting!" Healers jokes with him.

"Ah no, Colin – it's good news for a change."

We sit down and hush. The Gaffer starts with the important stuff: "Well boys, we have an investor. He's going to take over the club. That's the good news."

"What's the bad news, Gaffer?" Healy asks.

"The bad news is..." the Gaffer turns, in mock seriousness, to Denis: "...he wants you gone, Denis."

"That's double good news, Gaffer!" Healy shouts.

The lads all laugh at this, including Denis. But they're soon silent again, waiting for more.

"No – the news is there's an investor and I met him yesterday for two hours. His name's Tom Coughlan. He's going to come in. What he wants is…"

I have the feeling that our futures, and the club's future, are about to unfold from the Gaffer's lips.

"…a full-time club."

The relief in the room is palpable, although nobody moves.

"He has a brownfield site – hundreds of acres, out beyond here – but he doesn't want to go down that road. He wants to keep the pitch at Turner's Cross. He told me it's a fine stadium and the rent isn't bad. €40,000 a year: less than the club shop and the same as a four-bed semi-detached house in Dublin." The Gaffer laughs at his own joke before continuing…"He wants to come in and buy the Horseshoe Pub [the back end of which overlooks our home ground]. He's thinking of turning it into a corporate facility of sorts. I went through the figures with him; he didn't realise the administrative costs of running a club, the travelling expenses, etc. There's a discrepancy between what the club's been generating from the administrative side and what it's been spending, though I'm not blaming the people who've been running that side of things. There's just not enough coming in from that area.

"And he asked me about the creditors – which impressed me – so I told him they were mostly local people or companies that the club owed, from the likes of the Deanrock [the tavern that provides food to the players after training] to the program publishers, security at the games, and others. And he thinks that's wrong, what's happened to them. He says he wants to pay these people back. He's going to meet them and see if he can sort things out so we can work with them again in the future. He also wants to pay back the players whatever they're owed."

Everything sounds too sweet. We wait for the sting.

Denis butts in, "What kind of timeframe are we talking about, Gaffer?"

"He wanted to do it this week, and he tried to buy the pub but they're holding out on the price. But he is going to buy it this week."

The lads need more assurance and the Gaffer knows it.

"Also, lads, he's made a confidential agreement with the supporters to confirm he's coming in, and he wants them to get involved too. He wants to charge €400 for membership – so from 5,000 supporters that'd be €200,000 a year. But he's not looking for this overnight; he knows it might take years. Even so, he sees this as the way forward, with those fans getting a stake in the club."

While all this sounds great, experience tells me to wait. It isn't done yet. Does he have ulterior motives? What's in it for him? Before I even put these questions to the Gaffer he begins to address them.

"The thing is, lads, he's an engineer. He's got numerous hotels in Ireland and is working on a scheme in regard to the London Olympics. He's not short of cash and is living in a nice part of town."

Gamble says, "Ya, there's some nice houses up there alright, Gaffer."

"But he came in wearing a t-shirt and shorts, so I'm thinking he's not interested in the profile thing. He says he might get that solicitor, Gerald Keane, to front it for him as he's not interested in the exposure. He reckons an engineer likes to make his mark on a place – without publicity.

"He's football mad, but he says he's going to sponsor the Waterford Hurlers' homecoming also. So he's not in it to make money – he just wants to build the club and leave a mark on the place, on the city. He said he's not interested in Europe – it's not the end-game for him. So he's not gambling on us doing well in Europe to make his money back. He sees Europe as a bonus – something to work towards in the future. He really wants us to focus on winning things domestically. He wants a successful, vibrant club. So really it's all good news, lads."

A few smiles have emerged around the room.

"But we all know Mick wants us to go back to part time, don't ya Mick?"

Mick laughs.

The Gaffer continues, "I *know* we're going to win something this year and I want us to beat this lot tomorrow night."

There's no clear end to the meeting. Kearney makes a joke, the boys laugh and we walk out into the sun to get on with training.

The pitch is perfect today. The grass is freshly cut and rolled, and everything seems great again. Biscuits takes the warm-up, during which Kearney and I agree that we're not sure we should believe it. We decide to wait until it's done.

During the warm-up Gamble confides in me and Muz that Hartlepool have been onto him, but he told them he'll be staying at Cork unless the club goes to pot.

We play games of roughly 8 v 8, no conditions. I'm with the greens and we're full of good, ball-playing, experienced lads. We're the stronger side and we clean up. Crazy Daz, who's with the whites, angrily gives out: "Who the f*** picks these teams every week?!"

The lads are generally flying, though.

Young Timmy does well for the whites; he turns Muzza, who then completely hacks him down. The Gaffer, reluctantly, gives him a free. Then a minute later Mick Devine hacks him down and there's no free.

"I gave you the last one, Timmy," is the Gaffer's response to Timmy's plea.

It's a hard school for young players at this club; they don't have much time to try and get in the team before they're deemed 'not up to it' and shown the door. I assume it's the same with most clubs at this level. Timmy's been showing his ability for a while, but he needs to break through soon.

A Tipperary native, Timmy came to us in about 2007 having done his apprenticeship at Celtic for a few years. I think he's still reeling from the fact that it didn't work out for him over there. He's still trying to reinvent the game in his head – or rather his place in the game. He's suffered a setback at a young age, and it remains to be seen whether he's got a future in the game. As a striker his finishing needs improving, and he needs to concentrate more and stick up for himself too. But he's got power, a good touch and great ability, and he's still very young. He could be a very good player if he just tunes in a bit more.

Training finishes and the Gaffer calls us for a huddle, and then we go in to talk about tomorrow's game. He wants our full-backs to push onto their wingers and let our centre-halves deal with the space behind us, particularly as we're at home. He turns to Murph and me and asks if we know what he means.

We nod.

Afterwards I speak to the Gaffer about the new investor.

"It's good news, Hogs," he says. "A confidentiality agreement and some practical, common-sense plans."

"Sounds great," I say.

In the shower, Muzza, Lordy and Kearney all agree that it's best not to believe anything until we're getting fully paid again and the chairman's picture is in the paper.

But the good news and sunny weather are nice for a change.

Chapter Six

Arkaga Spending and Policies: A Player's Perspective

The new owners had gradually taken over the running of the club from locally based chairman Brian Lennox in 2007, and money was soon pouring in like never before. There was a sense of something major happening at the club – something new.

Lennox, joint-owner of the famous Cork fish-and-chip shop *Jackie Lennox's*, had sometimes been derided by City fans for being over-conservative, but in general he had proved a popular chairman – as demonstrated in a characteristically cheeky chant: *Who needs Abramovich, Lennox sells lots of chips... Who needs Ambramovich, Lennox sells lots of chips...* (to the tune of 'La Donna è Mobile' from Verdi's *Rigoletto*).

Lennox had alerted the players to the takeover, but we thought it was idle talk until Arkaga's Jim Little turned up at Bishopstown. Little was a tall, gaunt North American who, he told us, was here to front Arkaga's interest in Cork City – with help from Lennox to make the transition a smooth one. Little's lasting impression on the players was the way he said, "I'm in it for the *long haul*" in a very nasal American accent… and then promptly moved to Swindon Town FC.

He was replaced by Aidan Tynan, a former CEO of the Irish Greyhound Association who would become Arkaga's main point of contact with the players.

In meetings (first with Little and later with Tynan) the players were constantly told, in no uncertain terms, that the new owners of the club were seriously loaded. They were, we were told, 'people who invested in big companies around the world'. We were assured that this was the club to be at – that those getting offers from elsewhere, or thinking of moving, 'should stay or miss out'. They said the new owners were buying into

CCFC in order to start making a cultural impact; they had ideas about putting something back into society and saw investment in the club as a way of doing this.

I never quite understood what this meant or where they were coming from. An investment company whose main aim was to put back into society? What exactly was in it for them?

In any event, as players at that time we weren't overly concerned by any of these issues. We were happy enough in the knowledge that they were here to make the club grow stronger, on and off the pitch – and they were absolutely emphatic on this. They had plenty of money; there would be new facilities, new players... a fully professional outfit. These were the kind of changes that League of Ireland players and fans normally only dream of, so naturally we were all delighted with the plans.

Little and Tynan also spoke of how they wanted to build a multi-use stadium, possibly to use for other Cork events as well. Tynan compared our training pitch in Bishopstown to the bad turf of the old greyhound track in the city centre. He spoke of how greyhounds' feet were often injured on bad surfaces; he knew what it meant to train on a bad surface, and he knew the benefits of a good one. Players were not convinced by his expertise in this regard, nor delighted with the comparison, but it was not an issue. This club was moving somewhere worth going to, and that's all that mattered to us.

from the *Cork Independent*, January 2008

CITY TO ANNOUNCE POSSIBLE SITES FOR NEW STADIUM DEVELOPMENT

An announcement regarding the possible sites under consideration for the building of Cork City FC's proposed new stadium is expected by the month's end. While Cork City General Manager Aidan Tynan refused to comment on the development, a source within the club confirmed to the Cork Independent that an announcement on the club's '10 year plan' can be expected by the end of January. It is believed the club's new owners, venture capital firm Arkaga, have earmarked a number of sites for the development of the 20,000-seater stadium, with Cork Con's ground in Ballinlough and sites at Black Ash and Bishopstown being suggested as possible early favourites for the club's relocation. At a meeting earlier in the year, Tynan outlined the club's plans for the multipurpose stadium which will also incorporate bars, gyms and five- to seven-a-side pitches. The new stadium will also be capable of staging large-scale concerts, a key factor in Arkaga's plan to significantly reduce the club's current operating deficits. The club are said to be looking at 15 acres close to the city centre to house the development. According to the owners, the club will need to be generating annual profits in the region of €1.5 million by five years' time in order to support the investment, which is expected to cost up to €40 million.

Meanwhile, speculation is mounting over former city favourite and current Reading FC striker Kevin Doyle. Reports in the UK suggest the Irish International could be the subject of a €12 million bid from Chelsea in the January transfer window. The move, if it goes through, will net City €1.2 million.

~

Admittedly, in his bullish way Tynan *did* make progress, by bringing about some immediate changes that were much welcomed by the players. His ideas were clearly motivated by an ambition to make the club look and feel like a fully professional outfit.

Firstly, proper dinners were organised for the players after training each day for the first time since I'd been at CCFC. Before, Noelle Feeney – long-time supporter of the club and a self-appointed 'mother hen' to the playing squad – had sporadically and colourfully fulfilled the role of part-time chef. But for the most part, due to lack of finances and facilities, the best that could be served up had been beans on toast.

Rico had been pushing for regular decent food for the players for some time; in his view, allied with rest and recuperation, it was an essential part of the life of a full-time pro. (Dolan, for his part, had organized sandwiches after training.) The players, during one of many meetings with Tynan to outline and discuss the future of the club, now requested regular dinners after training.

So, after attempting in vain to develop a kitchen at the dilapidated Bishopstown ground, Tynan had arranged for the players to get food every day from a pub and restaurant in Togher (The Deanrock). The people there were happy to see us, and the players were delighted with the food and hospitality.

Another change for the players involved the laundering of training gear. Again, for the first time in my CCFC experience, our training gear was to be taken from us after each session and laundered by the club. This meant that on arrival for training every day our gear was ready for us. All a player had to do was collect his gear, which was folded together with his squad number on it, from the kit room down the hall from the dressing room. Tynan organised this firstly by employing the services of the local launderette (The Lough Launderette) that had been washing our match-day kit for years. He then set about buying washing machines for the club in order to minimise the long-term cost.

The food and laundry changes were in line with what Dolan and Rico had always envisioned, and most of our players has already experienced these things at English clubs. Even though they were small changes, they were significant. Some might argue that the provision of these basic everyday services represents a mollycoddling of players – and there may be some merit in that view. However, I noticed significant improvements in the psychology of our players. Now that the club was acting professionally the players were pushed, almost subconsciously, into behaving more professionally themselves. For the players these changes confirmed that Arkaga meant business – that the club was going in the right direction and that full-time professional football in Ireland was about to develop and mature.

There were significant changes away from the football side of things, too. New members of staff were appointed to mirror the administrative structure of overseas clubs. The club shop was moved to a prominent position in the City; a deal with new sponsors Hummel was announced; and the shop was filled with CCFC merchandise to an extent never seen before.

Along with these positive developments, somebody somewhere decided that a change of club crest was required. How much money was spent changing to a new, swishier crest I don't know, but I personally didn't like the move. What were the new owners trying to do? I wanted to feel a part of the club I'd supported while I was growing up, not some new club. The new crest was nice, but the old one was better in my opinion. Maybe I didn't have the marketing nous of the new owners or their advisors, but to me it seemed like money down the drain.

At some point in 2007 Arkaga also decided to change the way players would be paid. Instead of a base rate per week, Tynan began to negotiate players' contracts towards a performance-related rate. Thus players were told that their base rate would be reduced, but that if they were picked and played well, bonuses would take them above what they would have previously earned. For example, if you were on €600 per week (net) before the new owners came in, you would now be on something like €400 or €500, plus an appearance bonus of €100 per game and goal bonuses worth, say, €100. If you played more than one game in a week, and scored a few goals in each, you could earn significantly more than before. Thus high performers would be rewarded – at least that was the idea.

While most of us previously had some kind of bonus clause in our contracts, they hadn't consisted of such a high proportion of our earnings. The players saw some merit in these changes, designed as they were to reward success on the pitch. They would also reduce the risk of players sitting back on large contracts and not putting in the effort to play well or win trophies.

However, Tynan was only able to negotiate this performance-based scheme with new players and those whose contracts were ending in or around 2008. Thus players like myself (my contract was for two years, 2007 to 2009), who were on older contracts that were still effective for another season or so, were not subject to the reduced base rate or the new bonuses.

This discrepancy significantly undermined the new policy, as did the introduction of other dubious bonuses. A certain centre-forward, Mr Denis Behan, alerted us at some stage to the fact that his new contract allowed him to be in receipt of a 'clean sheet bonus' while sitting on the bench. (A clean sheet bonus is paid to a player when their team doesn't concede a goal in a match.) There's an argument that all players on the team, including centre-forwards, are responsible for the attainment of a clean sheet; indeed a forward – in keeping possession at vital times, in chasing and harrying opposition defenders, in making important tackles and in actually coming back and defending – may often play a crucial role in keeping a clean sheet. Whatever the merits or otherwise in that argument, it's hard to find any logic in someone getting a clean sheet bonus while sitting on the bench for the entire match.

The idiocy and injustice of such a bonus was compounded when considered from the point of view of a player such as myself, who might've left the field of play exhausted from his efforts but, being on a pre-existing standard contract, was not eligible for this 'reward'. Meanwhile Denis (or whoever) would stir from the bench and be rewarded for other players' endeavours.

"Well done lads," Denis would say to the exhausted back four, with a smile on his face.

Despite the beneficial changes they'd made, this situation highlighted – to the players, at least – that

Arkaga (or their representatives) lacked an understanding of the intricacies of professional football. Unfortunately the players and football staff were to become increasingly familiar with the new owners' ignorance.

Goal bonuses were another difficulty. These had, of course, existed pre-Arkaga, but to a lesser extent. While I hadn't had them in any of my previous contracts (although Brian Lennox did offer me a free bag of chips after a particularly tasty last-minute winner against Derry in 2003), a lot of the lads enjoyed goal bonuses in their contracts. During negotiations in 2007/08 Tynan increased goal bonuses significantly – to the point where they could make up a much higher proportion of a player's earnings – in keeping with Arkaga's policy of rewarding high performance.

While this may sound, in theory, like an effective 'results-based strategy', in practice it had the effect of players taking shots from all angles and almost fighting over who was to take penalties or free kicks.

It's well known that almost every successful centre-forward is greedy by nature, but the very best are able to integrate this instinct with effective and visionary team play, which, when supported by good players, can result in the most attractive and free-flowing football imaginable. Think Marco van Basten and Holland at Euro '88.

In my opinion it was questionable, at best, whether some of our forwards needed any added incentive to try and score. While I wouldn't suggest the players on our team were necessarily playing on their own for entire games, there were moments during those first few months of 2008 when I suspected speculative efforts – and especially secondary and further speculative efforts at goal – were inspired by financial gain at least as much as by a genuine desire to score a goal. This was an unhealthy development in a team that had become known for free-flowing and attractive team play over the preceding few years.

On top of changes to individual contracts, the new owners also introduced increased 'team bonuses'.

Tynan promised that the entirety of any winnings awarded to the club (by the FAI or by the competition's sponsors) for any silverware won or league standings achieved was to be divided among the players and the players only. This was a new and potentially lucrative offer; players were very happy to agree to lower base-rate contracts with these team-based bonuses, and individual bonuses, in their sights. Prior to this, they had received some kind of cut from the winnings awarded for winning a competition, but rest assured – they had never been given the full pot.

Tynan announced this 'entire winnings to the players' idea to journalist Noel Spillane, and it was soon published in the local paper. So it was that when we won the FAI Cup in November 2007 we were entitled to receive the full amount of winnings, to be divided among the players. However, in the early months of 2008 we had still not received any of this bonus, and rumours started to reach the players that Tynan was not going to stick to his promise. So a meeting was organised to discuss the matter.

Players had decided that captain Dan Murray, vice-captain Joe Gamble, and myself (as a legal student) would attend on their behalf; PFAI representative Stephen McGuinness also agreed to join us. On arrival into Tynan's office above the club shop in Daunt Square, it was clear that the guy was not happy with us. He was particularly unhappy with Muzza (because of Muzza's 'two fingers to the board' comment following the cup final), whom he verbally attacked on a number of occasions. Muzza remained admirably composed, and Gamble and I said very little as McGuinness tried to calm Tynan down and keep things from completely overheating.

Eventually Tynan offered us a significantly reduced proportion of the winnings, stating that he wanted to divide the remainder among the administrative staff for all their good work. We took some time outside to consider the offer; McGuinness advised us that if we wanted to we could hold out for the full amount, but we decided to compromise and accept the offer for the sake of the season ahead. The meeting ended in a decidedly cold manner, but at least we could move on.

So although the new performance-based contracts may have had some theoretical merit, their design and application left a lot to be desired. Arkaga and their CEO were new players in a market they hadn't experienced before; it was only natural that their learning curve would be sharp and they'd make mistakes. Money was clearly wasted. However, given Arkaga's self-proclaimed long-term plan, and their equally well-stated bountiful resources, players were confident that these mistakes would be ironed out in time. And Arkaga's representatives kept reminding us that they were in this for the *long haul*.

There were certainly improvements, both on and off the field, that were to be commended by any player that wanted the club to challenge other full-time clubs, both domestically and in Europe. However, Arkaga, for whatever reason, did not stay for the long haul and decided to cut their losses halfway through 2008; and when they left, the club owed roughly €1.3 million –

of which €360,000 was owed to the Revenue and the rest to local businesses and other suppliers.

Thus the changes that had helped us to become more professional eventually caused damage to local businesses (many of whom were left with unpaid bills) and effectively put the club into the Irish financial equivalent of intensive care: examinership.

The debts were put on hold, and a court-appointed examiner found himself in the unenviable position of having to deal with a wage bill – for players and staff – which matched that of a full-time UK or overseas club. He also had to make decisions on all of the other commitments that the club had made under the control of Arkaga, as well as on debts due and owing, in order to try and keep the club alive.

from the *Irish Times* 'Business This Week', March 27th 2009

Almost six out of ten companies operating in the state offer performance-related pay, with 63% saying such schemes are an effective motivational tool, according to a new report (IBEC's biannual human resources management survey of 298 organisations). Among companies where such schemes were viewed as ineffective, the problem was usually in the scheme design.

Chapter Seven

8th September to 5th October 2008

Monday 8th September

In his pre-match talk before we play Derry, the Gaffer tells us that certain people who are interested in taking over the club are at the match tonight.

"Things are happening for the better, boys," he says.

There's a good crowd so maybe we'll be paid something. Darragh Ryan scores and I'm delighted for him; Denis is hacked down in a scandalous tackle and stretchered off. We concede a late goal.

League of Ireland: Turner's Cross, Cork
Cork City 1–1 Derry City

The Gaffer's disconsolate afterwards. "We'll look at it tomorrow boys," he says.

In the circumstances, though, I feel the most important thing was not to lose.

Thursday 11th September

Today Sully takes some of the training, which is great to see. Lawrie's back from England also, but he's staying in the 'house of horrors' – a house in the outskirts of Cobh that has no running water, put up by the club. We ask Denis about his injury and he reckons he'll be fine once the stitches are out.

"Our wages are back up to 50% tomorrow, boys!" says Mick, who's found this out from Biscuits. Later, Stephen McGuinness (PFAI rep) rings each of us to see what we're owed.

Friday 12th September

No sign of 'No Show Joe' at training this morning. Kearney rings him a few times but there's no answer.

"Maybe he's gone to St. Pat's?" jokes Lawrie.

We train for an hour and then, with the Gaffer, we look at the late Derry goal on TV. He points out what we could have done better.

After the video session I go to the gym to do some core work. Crazy Daz Murph is checking his wages slip.

"50% wages in – get in there!" He's delighted as he's also heard that the potential new investor has bought the pub, and there's been something on *Red FM* about a bid for the club, too.

Saturday 13th September

In the first twenty minutes of the cup match Derry are zipping it about and they're well on top. We're chasing shadows. I'm wearing new boots and I blame them for my not moving as well as usual. But soon we improve and I do a few good things – tackles, etc – and forget about the boots. The Shed End starts singing a song about me that they bring out occasionally. It may be ungrateful to say so, but it's a very annoying song and I've never liked it; the players know this and they jibe me by singing it to get on my nerves. However, as the crowd only seems to sing it when I've done something good, I'm starting to appreciate it.

Then we score. Crazy Daz is a big ox of a guy who dribbles surprisingly well for someone of his size; he's very hard to stop when he's coming at you because he runs with such power. He goes through two of their players before slotting it into the bottom right with his left foot.

The second half is dull enough as things are tight, and Derry don't create much until the very end. There's only a minute left when their striker, Farren, makes a run from my area behind the centre-half next to me, and is found by a lovely pass by their creative midfielder, Higgins. Mick comes out quick but clashes with Farren and the ref points to the spot. They score the peno.

I'm at least partially responsible for the goal, but I already know Mick'll bear the brunt of the blame afterwards. I can tell from the Gaffer's demeanour on the sideline; he's not blaming me.

After that Healy has two great chances but just can't score at the moment. He rounded two or three of their players for the first opportunity but shot poorly, and then he missed with a header. Game over.

FAI Cup: Turner's Cross, Cork
Cork City 1–1 Derry City

The Gaffer's upset afterwards. He explodes at the referee and has to be manhandled away by some of the lads. In the dressing room he turns to Mick and asks whether it a peno. Mick doesn't think so, but some of the boys say it was so Gaffer blames Mick. It's a cruel game; Mick played well outside of that.

Afterwards Biscuits says to me, "Things just aren't going right for Mick at the moment. Sometimes you go through a phase like that, but you need to get out of it. The same happened to me when I was playing. It's an awful place to be, I can tell you."

I text Mick later to offer my support. Most players have been there – particularly defenders. I certainly have.

Monday 15th September

Even though Drogheda are the current League of Ireland champions, I find it hard to motivate myself for the game today. We hear they're also having money problems at the moment – which isn't much of a surprise as they have a huge squad of experienced, full-time players.

We arrive at the ground at a painfully early hour. The lads, perhaps because of this, start to mess like kids in the dressing room while the Gaffer's out on the pitch. It starts with Kearney, who's innocently chatting away to Daz Ryan when he gets hit in the head by a wine gum. It soon escalates into a full-scale food fight involving sweets, oranges, Lucozade and water. The lads are clever enough to clean up before the Gaffer gets back, but it certainly lightens the mood.

We start the match well and Crazy Daz scores another great goal with his left foot, but in the second half we tire and they get on top. They score, and are going for the jugular. Their manager, Paul Doolin, is jumping up and down on the line near me, commanding his players to push on for the victory. Twice they come close, but we hold on thanks to an incredible save by Mick.

Setanta Cup: Hunky Dorys Park, Drogheda
Drogheda United 1–1 Cork City

Thursday 18th September

The best thing about today was a fight between Kearney and Danny Murphy during a 7 v 7 match. Despite being former flatmates they dig the head off each other like true flyweights, landing loads of punches per second before being pulled apart by other players. Daz Ryan and I agree that if it was being judged on points it'd probably be a draw.

Afterwards the Gaffer tells us the examiner is to make a decision on a possible takeover soon.

Friday 19th September

Kearney and Murph are best buddies again this morning, and as we're warming up the lads take the piss out of them accordingly. Nulty explains, for someone who missed it, that it was "like *Rocky IV – here come the little people.*"

Saturday 20th September

Cobh's players are almost on strike, having been threatened with no pay until the end of the season. As it's a derby game a big crowd shows up, which will help their cause some bit. I know a lot of their players as they're ex-Cork City lads. I'd certainly prefer them not to go down, but at the moment it looks like they will.

We're under pressure as our fans will be venomous if we lose this one. Lawrie scores for us early on, but in the last two minutes Seany gives away a penalty and they score. They deserve it – we played s***. Healy and I take knocks.

If there were any doubts about it before now, in the dressing room after the match it's clear that the Gaffer is finding the late goals *very* hard to deal with.

League of Ireland: St. Colman's Park, Cobh, County Cork
Cobh Ramblers 1–1 Cork City

Sunday 21st September

I can't train with the injury. The Gaffer's not happy: he asks why we can't hold onto a lead and shows us games where we did so earlier in season. The boys can't answer. Crazy Daz is missing and nobody knows where he is; turns out his car, for some reason, went on fire and is out of action.

Monday 22nd September

We're at home to Cliftonville in the last group game
of the Setanta Cup. I meet Gamble and Kearney on the
pitch before the match; as I approach it's clear they're
not happy. They dejectedly tell me they've heard that
the new investor (Coughlan) is now not being put
forward by the examiner to take over the club, so
we're back to square one.

In the dressing room the Gaffer tells us he's giving
a few of the fellas who've played a lot of games
recently – including me – a rest. Sitting on the bench
is awful: you're torn between supporting the guy in
your position and wanting to cheer when he loses the
ball. The only good thing today is that I'm sitting next
to Woodsy, who's keeping us amused by trying to
wind up Mick, who's also on the bench. Every time
the second-choice goalkeeper (Nults) touches the ball,
Woodsy shouts: "Great play Nults!" or "Brilliant
Nults!" and we all, including Mick, have a laugh.

Setanta Cup: Turner's Cross, Cork

Cork City 4–1 Cliftonville FC

Final Standings: Setanta Cup, Group 1 – 2008

	Pld	W	D	L	GD	Pts
1. Drogheda United (R.O.I)	6	4	2	0	+10	14
2. Cork City (R.O.I)	6	4	2	0	+9	14
3. Cliftonville (N.I)	6	1	1	4	-5	4
4. Dungannon Swifts (N.I)	6	0	1	5	-14	1

Although we win 4–1 it's not enough to top the group, as Drogheda win their match 2–0. We'll therefore be playing the semi-final away from home, which is something the club could do without at the moment. The Gaffer's unhappy afterwards as Seany made a mistake again for their goal. I feel sorry for him; things are going wrong for him too at the moment.

The Gaffer made subs but didn't use Woodsy, who needs game-time. In the dressing room he tells me quietly that he thinks he might be finished now.

Gamble asks the Gaffer about the investor and the Gaffer says he doesn't know. Muzza says the rumour is that Coughlan has pulled out because the examiner was taking too long. We ask if we can meet the examiner again during the week; the Gaffer says he's in Germany but he'll try to set it up for as soon as possible.

Wednesday 24th September

This morning I tell Alex (the physio) that my neck is finally feeling OK and he pretends to faint in disbelief. He's under pressure – about ten of the lads are squashed into his room, all injured in some way or other.

I meet the Gaffer on my way back to the dressing room and ask him if there's any news from the examiner.

"There is, Hogs, and it's good." He gives the thumbs-up. "But I'll wait until we're on pitch to tell the lads."

Then he says, "You know we'll almost definitely be playing Derry in the next round of the Setanta as they beat St. Pat's last night?"

"Ya, I know, and I think we'll be ready for them, Gaffer."

We go our separate ways and I enter the dressing room to find the boys discussing the current situation.

Gamble says, "This is the same b****cks again. I need to know."

I tell them the Gaffer's going to talk to us about it, at which point we get a call to come out onto the pitch.

"Well, lads, here's what I know. Tom Coughlan is going to take over the club, and the rumour that he wasn't was only a smokescreen."

"Is that the 100% truth, Gaffer?" Gamble demands.

"It is, Joe. It's what I know. There was rumour of another investor, but he didn't want FORAS involved – and he also wanted a different manager, I think."

"When will we know for certain, Gaffer?" asks Murph.

"He wants to wrap it up as soon as possible. Hopefully by Monday."

"So that's your head on a plate on Monday, then, if it doesn't happen," Denis jokes.

"What's that, Denis?"

"Your head on a plate, Gaffer, if it doesn't go through."

The Gaffer still doesn't get it; the meeting peters out and everybody wanders off towards the balls.

Only ten players (including two keepers) train.

In the dressing room afterwards, Gamble declares: "This better not be b****cks again. I don't want to be f***ing messed about again!"

"You were sold the dream, Gamble," says Muzza sarcastically, and Joey concurs.

I go home and later get a phone call from 'mother hen' Noelle Feeney.

"Hi Hoggie love, I had to ring ya. The club is saved, love. Tom Coughlan's come in. I just got a phone call to tell me. Just wanted to tell you, love. And he's bought the pub and he's going to have a social club as well. I told him I'll help him with it."

"That's great news – thanks Noelle."

We'll see.

However, there's hope and I feel it. I'm going to try and focus more on my own performance, try to put more into it. I haven't been giving it the effort I should have lately, for whatever reason.

Friday 26th September

We're at home to UCD in the league. I haven't played in a while so I'm particularly nervous before the game. But I think the nerves are a healthy part of things, of preparation.

Before the match Healy comes into dressing room and tells us he's out for the rest of the season with a hair-line fracture of the shoulder. It happened in the match against Cobh. He'll be big loss.

League of Ireland: Turner's Cross, Cork
Cork City 2–0 University College Dublin

We do well to win as we're down to a very limited squad now.

Monday 29th September

We're training early (10am) as we're flying from Cork at 3pm to play tomorrow's FAI Cup replay in Derry. When I arrive in the dressing room from the gym there's a man shaking hands with all the lads as they walk in. The Gaffer follows me in and introduces him. It's Tom Coughlan – our new investor. Our white knight.

The lads all sit down and he begins to speak.

"The first thing I'll say is well done for getting through the Setanta Cup and the FAI Cup – and you're not doing too badly in the league, either. It's a great achievement, considering all that's been going on."

Then he raises his voice: "But the result against FC Haka wasn't good enough, lads."

He calms down again before continuing: "However, I'm delighted to be coming in and I can't believe it's actually happening after all this time. I want a strong club – a community-type club. I'm looking at the Barcelona model and the way their fans are shareholders in the club. I'll be working with FORAS with a view to giving the club over to the fans.

"The ground at Turner's Cross is fine but we need to work on the facilities generally. We want to create facilities that the crowds will enjoy coming out to, just like the dog track over the road. I'm also going to pay you back the money you're owed: it's a pill I have to swallow but that's the way it is. I think it'll create goodwill between us, so that's what I'm going to do. I'm not promising the sun and the stars, though. Things will have to be more realistic in future, but I do want the club to remain full time. Any questions, lads?"

None of the players dare to say anything, perhaps in fear that he'll change his mind.

Muzza eventually stands up: "Well, on behalf of the lads I just want to say thanks for coming in."

The Gaffer asks several questions about general stuff, and then Tom wishes us good luck for tomorrow night and leaves.

We get back to training and for the first time in a while we're able to properly focus on the football. Unfortunately the session is cut a few minutes short when Gamble hurts his knee after colliding with Lawrie. In clear agony he catches a ball in his hand and volleys it (using his good leg) away into the stand. Lawrie, thinking it's his fault, walks over to apologise but Joey says it was the ground that hurt his knee. Either way, the Gaffer thinks it's a good time to call a halt to things. He finishes with a speech that emphasises how important it is be switched on tomorrow.

Later we fly up to Dublin and get a bus to Derry from there. Joey, who doesn't like flying, gets a train and meets us in Dublin – and inevitably he's late.

Tuesday 30th September

The pre-match meal is horrible and the lads aren't happy. But it's forgotten about as we wind through the streets of Derry, over the wide River Foyle and through the built-up estates with murals on the walls before climbing up and up again to the Brandywell. Of all away venues this is the one I tend to enjoy most, and perhaps because of that I tend to play well here. Derry have a vociferous and colourful support and – almost always – a decent team. There's also a profound sense of history about the place.

Most of the lads don't like it: in addition to the 1,000km return journey there's also quite a noticeable hill on the pitch, facing down into one goal. But there's a hill at Turner's Cross too – it's just less noticeable.

Today the match lives up to the occasion. The place is packed and the Derry fans are in full voice. We're on our game and so are they; it's a cracking cup tie.

However, I'm more concerned with their left-winger, Niall McGinn. I've marked him before in Cork and I know he has ridiculous pace. He uses it to his advantage by kicking the ball ahead of him and me and then running onto it. This guy's quicker than most guys I've marked.

The trick with pacy wingers is normally to keep them turned the other way, and today is no different. If I can keep him facing his own goal I feel he can't hurt me. However, Derry are good at switching the ball from one side to the other and they do this to create space and move our back four around. The 'switch ball' also allows McGinn to receive the ball facing our goal – and facing me.

When the ball's on the other wing and Derry have it, I have to 'tuck in' close to my nearest central defender (but not so close that I lose touch with McGinn) and, crucially, stay inline with him (or a step

ahead of him) so as not to play behind the other lads
and allow Derry strikers to play onside behind my
fellow defenders.

In this position I'm the one with the best view of
the back four as I can see everything when I look
across. I therefore have to talk now more than ever.

"Sully, he's on your back... He's dropped off your
left side, Muz... He's coming across, Muz – I'm
passing him... Keep the line, Murph – stay up!"

It's particularly difficult to be heard amid the noise
of a big crowd, but it has to be done.

As soon as Derry switch the ball I have to deal with
it arriving to my man. I need to travel from inside,
next to my nearest central defender, to outside near
McGinn. The lads have to move across accordingly
and tighten everything behind me. Murph, at left back,
will become the eyes now. As the ball's travelling to
McGinn I have to get close to him – hopefully before
it arrives at his feet. Muzza calls, "First touch, first
touch!" meaning I need to get close enough to take it
from him after his first touch.

My ability to do so depends on a number of factors: the quality, pace and trajectory of the pass to him; the quality of the player himself (whether he has a good first touch or not) and whether he's in form; and his pace versus mine. I'll have worked out a few of these things subconsciously on the way to the ground.

So McGinn is quicker than me; his first touch is good, but I feel I need to get at him now as he improves with subsequent touches. His second touch, I've noticed, is likely to put it past me and run. This is where he has the advantage. I therefore need to get close, look to nick the ball after or on his first touch – or, even better, challenge as the ball arrives.

If I can't get there as the ball arrives I'll position myself to show him down the line, reducing his ability to take his first touch and knock the ball straight past me. I'll be in a half-turned sprinting position, giving myself a yard's head start in case he just plays it ahead of me and runs.

These decisions will inevitably have to be made in a millisecond while the ball arrives. Sometimes, when you've got a winger in your pocket, *you're* effectively the one making decisions for *him*, as he's thinking about your arrival more than he's thinking about the ball. Tonight, in my opinion, McGinn and myself are neck and neck. He's getting joy, but only in areas that I'm allowing him – such as on the inside (nearer-centre of pitch), where my midfielders are of help to me. I often brief the midfielders before a match – or they might brief me – on the dangerousness of a winger and the need for help from them if he goes inside. On the other hand, if he goes outside (nearer the sideline) he's my sole responsibility; I'll try to tighten the space between myself and the sideline as he comes at me. A trap of sorts. Then tackle if needed – although the preference would be to stay on my feet.

If he does take me on then ideally I should stand up, attempt to block all crosses and, most importantly, not 'get done' by a winger faking to cross and then cutting in as I'm trying to block. If he manages to do this, my nearest central defender (Sully) will have to decide whether to (a) stay where he is and let the winger shoot or cross; (b) charge across, leaving the striker unmarked, to try and block the winger's shot or cross completely; or (c) a bit of both, whereby he'll wait with the striker until the winger's in a very dangerous shooting position, and then come across in the hope that the delay has allowed time for the other central defender (Muzza) to get across and pick up his man, with the other full-back (Murph) moving across to take Muzza's man.

This works best when Murph has seen it all early and told the two lads to go across. If there's no talk – due to negligence or the unpredictable nature of the danger – one of the defenders may not move across, or both will go to same man. This highlights the importance of prompt talk form the furthest full-back, and forms the basics of defending at this level.

Today we're 'switched on' at the back and working together smoothly. I do OK; McGinn does me once or twice but Sully, Muzza or our midfielders are able to cover, and I do my corresponding covering for them. My ability to go forward is limited by McGinn's pace:

I know if I'm the wrong side of him I'll have a problem getting back on the right side closer to my goal, particularly if they're counter-attacking. So today I'm more conservative than usual, which reflects our team strategy in general.

We're successful enough to hold them to a goalless draw and the game goes to extra time and penalties. The Gaffer examines us in the middle of the pitch, trying to see who's up for taking one.

After a brief pep talk, all of us huddled around him, he asks, "So... who fancies it?"

Denis is first to volunteer: "I will, Gaffer."

"OK then, Denis – you're number one." The Gaffer scribbles in his notebook.

Sully says he'll take one.

"OK Sully – you're number two."

Crazy Daz, standing behind Gaffer, says, "I'll take one, Gaffer."

But the Gaffer doesn't seem to hear him and continues: "Who wants to take the third?"

Kearney puts his hand up to volunteer. "OK Liam. Now then, two more lads?"

Crazy Daz, struggling to get the attention of the Gaffer, puts his hand up like Liam did and says, "I will, Gaffer!"

But the Gaffer pointedly turns away from him and looks at the others without saying anything.

Muzza steps in: "I'll take one."

"Right. That's four – just the last one now, lads?"

Crazy Daz, coming around in front of Gaffer, clearly states, "I will, Gaffer."

The Gaffer delays, and then Danny Murphy volunteers.

"OK Danny – you're fifth. Then you, Daz, if it goes to sudden death."

A few looks are exchanged among the lads as they acknowledge, without speaking, that the Gaffer has pulled a fast one on Crazy Daz. For whatever reason, he didn't want him taking a peno.

In any event Denis misses the first one, blazing it over, and Derry score all theirs. The lights go out, the crowd leaves, and we're no longer holders of the FAI Cup.

FAI Cup: The Brandywell, Derry

Derry City 0–0 Cork City (Derry go through on penalties)

We leave the ground at 11pm and get back in Cork for 5.40am. It's never nice losing in Derry as you've too long to think over things in your head on the way home.

Thursday 2nd October

We're down to twelve players (including two keepers) in training as Denis, Alan O'Connor and Daz Ryan all got injured up in Derry. After a light session the Gaffer raises the issue of food for tomorrow's away match at Galway.

"Who wants the same as the other night [pasta and boiled chicken] for pre-match?"

Nobody puts their hand up.

"How about spaghetti bolognaise instead, so?"

There's a big cheer.

Friday 3rd October

We've got an old, 1970s-style bus this morning. It smells and there's a fly buzzing about my window. I'm not happy. As the injuries are mounting up we've got two young boys from the youths or under-20s on the bus. I don't know who they are. Normally I'd make an effort to introduce myself, but this morning I can't be bothered as I'm tired and cranky and I don't want to travel to Galway to play a match – especially after the round-trip to Derry a few days ago. What have we got to play for anyway, now that ten points have been taken off us? Fourth again?

The Gaffer's booked us into a hotel in Galway for a few hours so we can get some sleep during the day and have pre-match. Later, at the dinner table, the boys are talking about the club's financial situation and how people need to get their contracts sorted. Murph says he's received a letter that says as a preferred creditor he's being offered 65%, or something like that, of what he's owed. He tells us there's a creditors' meeting tomorrow.

Gamble says the Deanrock (who provided our dinners after training) have been offered 7% of what they're owed: that's €900 rather than €15,000. We agree they can't accept that.

"What happens if a few creditors don't accept?" someone asks.

Nobody really seems to know.

The Gaffer calls the team meeting and springs a few surprises. Timmy's in for his first start, playing in front of me on the right wing; Woodsy starts at left-back and Murph's at left-wing.

Their winger, Jay O'Shea, has just been called into the Ireland under-21s and is attracting interest from all over the UK with his recent performances. Woodsy – who's about 57, part time and on his last legs – will be marking him. He'll no doubt do a job, but I'm thinking maybe we should have put Murph (who's in his prime) on him with Woodsy in front.

We start OK but then deteriorate. I play one good ball then three bad ones. Some City fans have travelled up and are sitting near me on this side of the stadium, and after my second bad ball I hear someone explode from the crowd behind me: "For f***'s sake, Hoggie! Come on, for f***'s sake!"

I can't blame the guy, but even so I feel like turning around and telling him to f*** off.

We come in 2–1 down at the break and the Gaffer's raging. My head's down and I'm finding it very hard to be up for the second half. I haven't felt so low for a long time and would prefer to be anywhere but here.

Biscuits is trying to gee us up in his Welsh accent: "For f***'s sake, come on! Yee have to be up for it and at them!" It feels like we're in a Welsh episode of *Dangerous Catch* and the ship's going down.

Maybe it really is.

Gamble adds, sombrely, "Boys, this is the worst we've been. Come on to f***!"

Muzza's saying the same, but I can't even lift my head I feel so bad.

The Gaffer makes no changes and we trudge back out into the cold. In the second half we get on top and I feel better. I start shouting at the people around me, but with fifteen minutes or so to go one of their strikers gets played in and Mick charges out, clashes head-on and brings him down. The ref waves play on and they score, making it 3–1 to Galway. Mick's out for the count when I get to him. Galway players run past us, celebrating, as we gather around Mick. He partially wakes but then tells us to "just leave me sleep." He's stretchered off. I hope he's OK.

We score late on and push for an equaliser, but it's no good. We lose 3–2 and trudge off.

League of Ireland: Terryland Park, Galway
Galway United 3–2 Cork City

The Gaffer's not happy at all. We get changed quickly and I go home with Woodsy, who drove straight up from work. On the way back we agree these are scary times.

Chapter Eight

Interview with Brian Lennox, August 2013

Neal Horgan: How did you become chairman of Cork
City Football Club?

Brian Lennox: Well, I might mention – and it is
perhaps apt – that I actually became chairman on
Aprils Fool's Day, 2002. But I first got involved with
the club in an official capacity in 1995. Of course, I
had been an ardent fan of the club, and a season-ticket
holder, for many years. My father Jackie had been a
prominent player with Cork Athletic in the 1950s, and
my family was steeped in the history of the game in
Cork. In fact my grandfather, Cornelius F Lennox,
died when attending a Munster derby match between
Waterford and Cork Hibernians on the 8th of March
1971.

Anyhow, at some stage in 1997 I was invited to the launch, at a local hotel, of a lottery idea to raise funds for the club. The board of the club at the time had decided to bring some of the sponsors together and asked them to get involved in selling the lottery tickets. During this meeting I cheekily asked how I could become a member of the board rather than merely selling the lottery tickets.

I was – and still am – a partner in a successful family business in Cork City: Jackie Lennox's Fish & Chip Shop and Takeaway. In any event I got a phone call the next day inviting me to come onto the board, and I said yes. The very next day I received another call from one of the board members saying the club was folding, that there was a dispute within the board itself. In the end some changes were proposed and I was suddenly made vice-chairman. I remained in this position for about five years before taking over control on my own.

NH: Why did you take it over on your own?

BL: There had been differences of opinion about which way the club should be going. I decided I wanted to move the club in a certain direction and assumed full control in order to do so.

NH: What direction was that?

BL: Well, I remember a match that we played in Europe against a team from Latvia. We should've beaten them well but we lost the match. On the plane home nobody seemed too bothered, but I was pissed off. I thought surely we could do better than this. From that point on my goal was to make the club more professional. At the time the club seemed happy to stay in the top half of the table and saw European matches as a bonus; I wanted us to actually win trophies and to progress in Europe – not to just turn up for the pints.

So I made some changes straight away: firstly, I changed the colour of the club back to the green and white of the Cork Hibernians sides that I'd enjoyed watching when I was growing up in the 70s. Green and white – not red – in my opinion are the traditional colours of Cork soccer. Then I pushed the idea of Friday-night football, and for the matches to start at 7.45pm, which was now possible as lights had been brought into Turner's Cross for the first time by the FAI/MFA [Munster Football Association]. We also introduced new players.

Liam Murphy was the manager of the club when I took over, and he was a shrewd operator financially. The players weren't paid very much and were mainly part time, but we did OK in the league – without threatening to win anything. The gates were, in the main, capable of covering the wages. Then, at the end of the 2003 season, Liam had had enough of managing the side. So he decided to move away from team management and operated more in an advisory capacity from then on – a role he would fulfil to my great satisfaction as I knew I could trust him implicitly. I then advertised for a new, full-time manager and got a lot of responses.

NH: Why did you want a full-time manager?

BL: I knew that you needed a full-time manager if you had full-time players, otherwise those players were likely to spend their spare time in the bookies, or worse. Shelbourne had been dominating the league and had more full-time players than anyone else; I wanted to be able to compete with them and beat them. It would subsequently come to light that Shel's were spending beyond their means, but nobody knew that at the time.

Bohemians were also doing well and had full-time players too, so in 2002 I set a plan or targets for the next four years: fourth, third, second, and then domination. This nearly came to fruition.

NH: And things went well – *very* well – for a period?

BL: Yes they did. We would in fact finish fourth, third, second and then first in successive years up to 2005. But domination, unfortunately, didn't follow. European results also improved dramatically and really put us on the map. The money from Europe also helped us to become more professional: you could get, say, €120,000 from UEFA for merely playing in the first round, so I knew I could put, say, €100,000 into our preparations for the European away leg itself. This would involve chartering a plane and putting the squad in a top-notch hotel for a few days prior to the match. I could also afford to send the manager, Pat Dolan, on research trips to see our opposing side in the flesh in advance of our matches. He soon became adept at this – to the point that the lads knew which one of our opposing players was having a fight with his wife; which player wanted secretly to leave the club, etc. Pat was very thorough and it all helped us to progress. It helped push us towards becoming more professional in our own league on our return from Europe.

Our standards were improving – the players knew it, the fans knew it and the media soon found out. I actually used to reserve priority seats for the media to fly with us on our chartered plane on the trips to Europe; I wanted them to let everyone know we were a professional outfit now, and to get away from the idea that Europe was merely a piss-up.

Soon sponsorship doors started to open: more and more wanted to get involved with us. The sales of our jerseys went through the roof around the time of our successful European runs. I think we had the second-biggest-selling jersey in Ireland at one point – second only to Munster Rugby. We were appearing on the back pages of Irish newspapers, and were even making it into English soccer magazines. I would regularly take calls from English radio too.

Unfortunately this also meant that more scouts started to sniff around the club. Soon these vultures began to circle and land in Turner's Cross in higher numbers than ever before.

But I found we couldn't sustain the same success, in terms of publicity, in our own league. Some of the fans that came out and watched us play against Nantes, or Red Star Belgrade, weren't bothered to see us play against UCD or Bray. There's just not enough sexiness about the League of Ireland. I tried to fill the squad with characters that would keep the Cork public interested even if we were playing the lower teams in the league. I got lucky when Liam [Murphy] signed Georgy [O' Callaghan] and Johnny [O'Flynn]: they brought a sparkle.

By the time we won the league we had a team full of characters that the Cork public responded to, but even so, the gates couldn't quite support the wages of the better players we'd brought in. The sponsorship money did come in and help to some extent, as did television rights money and prize money, but it was more of a struggle to keep things ticking over with a better full-time team than it was with the part-time team that had existed when I first took over as chairman.

NH: Were other chairmen in the league in the same position as you?

BL: It was hard to know; I didn't really have many dealings with any of the other chairmen. When we did have dealings we were inevitably trying to outdo one another, to sign this player or that. We were competing with each other. The players were the ones that benefited from this, as they were able to negotiate better wages. But most of the chairmen, it turns out, were in over their heads financially.

NH: Were these chairmen from different backgrounds than you?

BL: No – they were probably from similar backgrounds. I know that Ollie Byrne [chairman of Shelbourne] had family that was steeped in the history of the game. I think he had a family business too, but I'm not sure. Liam Cody of Boh's [Bohemian FC] was also similar in those respects, I think. Derry's Jim Roddy was one chairman I did get on with, and Derry City FC was a club that seemed to get on with ours in every respect.

There were meetings in Dublin where all the chairmen would attend, and I was one that pushed for more regional meetings. The FAI move their AGM around the country these days, which I think is good.

NH: How did you get on with the FAI? Were they supportive?

BL: In general I got on very well with them. I didn't think they were really interested in our league, though – and I wasn't afraid to say it. I did have a particular falling-out with them at one stage over a remark made by the then manager of the Irish national team, as he'd said League of Ireland players needed to move to England to get into his team. This was contrary to everything I believed in; I felt we'd made such progress that it was no longer the case. They were good enough already. I'm still sure of that now, that they were good enough. Of course, if an English club signed them, all of a sudden they were selected for the Irish squad. But while playing for us the Irish manager wouldn't be interested. Did those few weeks change them so much as players? Obviously not. The message that comment sent to our best players was enraging, especially given all the work we'd done to raise standards here.

Players soon left and got into the Irish team. These included [Kevin] Doyle and [Alan] Bennett, and to a lesser extent [David] Meyler and Shane Long. *Of course* they left to play at bigger clubs on a bigger scale – but this was not the same as saying you *had* to leave to play for the Irish team. If you're good enough you should be chosen, full stop. Although Joe Gamble was eventually to get a cap whilst playing for us, I think the manager of the Irish team was still of the opinion that you had to move to England to get into the Irish squad. At the time, our league had five or six full-time teams; this shouldn't have been the case. It's different now, of course.

NH: How did you manage to pay for a full-time team?

BL: With great difficulty. We would have the gate money, sponsorship money and the possibility of prize money and European money. Television rights were another thing: at the time you were given around €15,000 by the broadcasters and the FAI for a domestic league fixture, although your gates would be affected. In Europe you could do your own deal, but when I took over the club was committed to a deal with a German company that would pay a standard annual fee for European broadcasting rights, no matter how many times you played in Europe – if at all. When it was signed up to, the board (or whoever) must've thought it was easy guaranteed money; they probably didn't envision a scenario where we were to play six or eight European games every year. When this happened, this deal meant we lost out on what we should have earned.

I remember, to his credit, Ollie Byrne – who wasn't restricted to any such deal – used to arrange to meet whoever it was he was drawn against immediately after the draw, wherever it took place. He would bring them to a meeting room upstairs and iron it out as soon as possible. He made it work for his club. But it didn't work out as it should have for us. I remember getting sight of what some of the better teams we played in Europe were earning from European and domestic TV rights, and it was on another planet compared to us. We just couldn't compete at that level, financially.

Still, on the domestic scene the prize money did go up substantially and I suppose that reflects the main contribution or support we got from the FAI in relation to any of this. In truth, though, I don't think the FAI were ready for us.

NH: What do you mean?

BL: We were becoming more successful than they'd imagined – to the point where we were a headache for them. All this new-found exposure meant they could no longer brush us under the carpet; they had to start thinking about how to deal with us and how to deal with the league. I felt like we were disturbing the comfortable status quo they had going for themselves. I think some in the FAI, and some in their regional branches, were under the impression that we were becoming too big for our boots. We were more of a burden for them when we were successful. That was my impression.

NH: Were the FAI interested in promoting a full-time league?

BL: I don't know. When they finally took over the running of the league in 2007 they promised more prize money, better TV deals and the like. I don't really know why they decided to take over the league at that point, or why it had taken them so long to do so.

NH: Outside of the FAI, did you receive any support from the government, from councillors or civil society?

BL: When we were going well we received numerous civic receptions in our honour. At these I would inevitably speak to some councillor or other about the possibility of help – perhaps in the provision a training ground – but sadly it never came to much in the end.

NH: So at some stage you decided to look for assistance?

BL: Yes. I knew where my level was. I knew we couldn't get to the next level with the budget I was operating on. I knew we'd need investment from outside to push it forward, that I couldn't push it any further on my own. I was also exhausted. I was working full time in my job as well as trying to be chairman of a full-time football club. It seemed like I would go straight from work to a football-related meeting and then straight back to work. It was wearing me out. And the costs of going full time had been substantial.

Also, everyone's mindset changed. Suddenly there was more waste. Little things were adding up: for example, Neale Fenn used to cut his socks at the ankle before every match so that he could wear his own ankle socks, as he felt more comfortable wearing them this way. He may have learnt that at Tottenham – I don't know. Anyway, it meant that he would need a new set for the next day. The other players saw this and soon they were doing the same. I watched Denis Behan recklessly kick balls away at training without attempting to retrieve them. Those balls cost €80 each.

This kind of unnecessary waste became more evident in other parts of the club too. There was a mentality that because we were full time we could act recklessly. But that was far from the truth. The increased costs associated with full-time football were substantial; everything from the provision of food after training to improved pre-season training camps, increased wage costs for a growing backroom staff... it all adds up.

NH: Do you think a full-time league needs bigger owners?

BL: Yes, you certainly need bigger pockets. And essentially there came a stage where I needed assistance from people with bigger pockets.

NH: Was there much interest?

BL: There was some initial interest alright, but the first credible approach was made through my solicitor, Olann Kelleher. He rang me and said he'd received a phone call from someone who was interested in buying the club, and would I meet with him. I was happy to meet with the man, so it was arranged that we'd meet at a hotel next to Cork Airport.

I brought Olann and my accountant with me; this man – who was Scottish – brought a whole entourage, including solicitors. He told me he had a holiday home in West Cork, a fondness for the League of Ireland, and had read all about us recently. He mentioned Arkaga in the meeting and I assumed he was the owner. He looked the part and my advisors agreed there might be something in this, so we agreed to meet again, this time in the Hayfield Manor Hotel just a few weeks later.

Again everything sounded rosy. He – or Arkaga – was seriously interested in buying the club and pushing it to the next stage. This Scottish man soon put me in touch with someone called Jim Little.

My first impression of Little was of a well-dressed, distinguished-looking American. I know it sounds silly now, but I became convinced that Jim Little was the guy behind Arkaga and that I was selling the club to him. After negotiations with Little had drawn to a close I announced to the fans in the middle of the pitch before a match that was being screened live on TV, with Little standing beside me: "This is Jim Little – owner of Arkaga."

Looking back, there were clues about Little that I should have spotted. He was around for a few weeks and we got to know him. We brought him to pubs to sample the local atmosphere, and some of us became aware that he would seldom buy a round of drinks. When it was his turn he would say all he had on him was his credit card, and we must have thought at the time that Little, being from the US or wherever, didn't realise the importance of buying a round once in a while when everyone else was buying them for you.

He also used to bum my cigarettes a lot. Looking back now, he probably just didn't have much money.

In any event, Little informed me that the plan was for me to stay on as acting chairman and have a say in how the club was run, and this alleviated many of my concerns. However, when the contracts were to be signed Olann pointed out that the name of the purchaser had changed from 'Jim Little' to 'Jim Little on behalf of Arkaga'. He said I should wait and find out more before signing, but I was anxious to get the deal done. I couldn't keep the show going financially; I was running out of time. I felt that if I was to remain acting chairman then at least I could deal with any problems in the first few months, as I would still have some control. So I signed the contract.

NH: What happened next?

BL: Well, a week later I was summoned to a meeting in the River Lee Hotel [formerly Jury's Hotel]. I was met by Denis O'Sullivan and Aidan Tynan, directors of Arkaga. They informed me that Jim Little was gone and that I was not to make any anti-FAI comments in match programmes or in the media. They were interested in an All-Ireland league and wanted to keep the FAI onboard. This all came as a sudden shock to me. It transpired later that the FAI had brought Jim Little to the US to watch Joe Gamble get his cap for

Ireland. I was surprised by this; I'd been chairman for five years and they'd never even given me a free ticket for a home Ireland match. They treated him like royalty. Clearly they, too, were hoodwinked.

NH: From your point of view, where did it go wrong with Arkaga?

BL: I know this'll sound egotistical, but one of the main problems was that they just didn't listen to anything I said. Whatever I advised them, they seemed to do the opposite thing. It became clear that they just wanted me to act as a trusted face or image for them, and that they had no interest in any of my opinions or in any of the knowledge I'd gained from being involved in the club for so long. Aidan Tynan soon announced to the fans that I was a non-executive director only and had no say in the club.

Tynan, as CEO, did many things that I advised him strongly not to do. For example, on meeting the players he agreed to pay them, in entirety, any prize money that was won – which I thought was ridiculous. I previously had a deal whereby the players would get a proportion of the prize money – say 50% – to be divided amongst them as they saw fit, and the players were happy with this. I told Tynan not to make his promise but he did it anyway and it was stupid. Afterwards the prize money increased and he had to try and back out of it. He was throwing money away.

We also had one or two other cases pending where I'd received strong legal advice that we had taken the right approach and would win the cases hands down, but Arkaga didn't want the bad press of a court case and just paid out the money. In my opinion they were reckless to do so.

NH: Did you see bad things coming down the tracks?

BL: Not really. I saw the mistakes they were making, yes. Then I noticed that Tynan went missing for a period. Nobody seemed to know what was happening. Then all of a sudden a guy takes over from Tynan and tells me the club has no money and asks me what we're going to do. This was Pat Kenny – he was a nice man, and he was convinced that the club was in serious trouble and that examinership should be considered. It was only at this stage that I discovered that the main man behind Arkaga was Gerard Walsh.

NH: Did you ever meet Walsh?

BL: I did meet him, but only once. It was around the time that Pat Kenny had stepped in and the club appeared to be in difficulty; after much effort, I eventually got hold of Walsh's mobile number and got into a texting conversation with him over the course a few weeks. It was very strange. The net point he made was that he had no money now and would I take over the club again.

I arranged to meet with him for the first and last time in the Imperial Hotel. Walsh told me that a lot of his finances were caught up in the Royal Bank of

Scotland, which had gone belly-up. Whether that was true or not I don't know.

NH: Do you have any regrets with regard to the way things turned out?

BL: Yes, of course – but maybe not in the way you think. When Arkaga wanted to come in I really didn't have any other options. FORAS had come to me with a proposal at some stage alright, but I didn't think it would work smoothly. Some of their members had been very critical of me at certain times; as such I didn't feel we could really work together – or at least I wouldn't have been comfortable with it. There were a few other people who'd been interested until they'd found out we didn't own Turner's Cross, at which point their interest had evaporated. There were one or two others... Tom Coughlan had been interested, but I didn't feel he knew what he was getting himself into, so I turned him away. So I was left with Arkaga, with myself as acting chairman to oversee the transition.

So yes – *of course* I wish it had worked out differently for the club. But I really had no other option at the time.

Chapter Nine

6th to 24th October 2008

Monday 6th October

It's early and there's just Dan Murray and myself in the dressing room when groundsman Jerry Kelly – who's sporting a particularly mucky pair of wellington boots – swaggers into the room and sits down with a loud sigh. When we ask him what's wrong he tells us there's a creditors' meeting today and rumour has it that at least one or two of them are not going to accept the offer.

"Which means the club can apply for a further thirty days to sort it, and if it's not sorted after that club will be liquidated. And that's not the only bad news," he adds. "Someone came last night, cut the bars of the fence over there with a bar-cutter and stole one of our lawnmowers. They must've dragged it off into a van: big, heavy thing it was. Luckily it didn't even work – it was a heap of s***," he says with a chuckle, before a sombre expression reasserts itself on his face.

Only ten players train. Biscuits takes it as someone says the Gaffer's daughter's in hospital. Biscuits, who is clearly from the old school of training, runs the hell out of us.

Later that day, up in Northern Ireland, Derry beat Linfield in the Setanta Cup to top their group. So we'll definitely be playing Derry (again) in the semi-final up in the North.

Wednesday 8th October

Myself and Lordy are late coming out of the gym this morning and we find the lads have already gone out onto the pitch for training. They're having a meeting; the players are huddled around the Gaffer and Biscuits. Lordy and I sneak in behind the lads so that the Gaffer, who is speaking, doesn't see us coming late.

He's on about the club. He looks grim.

"…all the other creditors have said yes but the Revenue have said no. If they say no again today – if the court decides it's not recoverable – the club could be gone."

A couple of the lads murmur, "For f***'s sake!"

Mathews continues: **"I don't know about this Coughlan fella either – he's giving me mixed feelings at the moment. I asked him for a budget plan for the future and he said he couldn't give it to me. He might want a part-time team. I don't know. But I think it's beginning to look that way, to be honest. He's keeping Pat Kenny on, so he's already going back on what he said about a salesperson and chief executive. So I don't know what's going to happen. The best we can do is sit him down and hold a meeting, if this goes through this week. I'll certainly be sitting him down with some bullet-point questions."**

Gamble pipes up, "Ya, we didn't grill him enough the last time, Gaffer."

Kearney adds, "If you think about it he said nothing specific, did he? We should make sure he pays us back our money before he comes in."

The Gaffer doesn't respond but continues, "Also, he told me he was going to make arrangements to pay back some of the creditors that'll be important to the club in the future. That would include UCC, Mayfield FC and the Deanrock. But he hasn't gone near them. That doesn't make sense to me, since he's bought the pub…"

"But *has* he bought the pub, Gaffer?" asks Dan Murray. "I heard a rumour that he hasn't, and that the price has changed because the joint owner of the pub died last weekend."

Dan has also heard from the PFAI that Coughlan's planning to offer terrible contracts to everyone.

"I don't know," Mathews says. "I suppose we'll have to wait until things go through and then see. Anyway, lads, I know it's difficult but we need to try and focus on Friday. We'll wait and see what happens with the rest of it – I just wanted to fill you in as best I can."

The players go about training without much of a grumble: perhaps we're becoming immune to it all...

As we leave, Denis says he's heard we're only getting 55% this weekend.

"Fellas who need to pay bills are going to be caught soon if this continues," he adds, dejectedly.

Dan Murray says to me, "I wish I'd gone to college like you, Hogs."

But I'm not sure whether he really means it.

Ever since the news circulated around the City that the club's in trouble, people have generally been sympathetic. I buy a DVD from Easons on Patrick Street and the lady serving me says, "I suppose you won't want any cash back with all your pay cuts, love?"

She laughs, and so do I.

"Ah, I hope it all gets sorted out for yee, though," she says warmly as I leave.

Other people are quick to tell you they think the players are to blame because of the high wages. Everyone seems to ask you about it; it soon gets tiring.

Thursday 9th October

No sign of the Gaffer this morning and we're all waiting around. Gamble threatens to take training – which would mean gym work consisting of nothing but squats – but then the Gaffer arrives, thank God.

Nulty whispers to me, "You know the club's in crisis when even the Gaffer's late!"

On the pitch and the Gaffer calls us over to him as he's walking towards us.

"Sorry about this, boys – I slept it in. Biscuits rang me fifteen minutes ago and I was still in bed."

But the lads don't mind. He tells us about our travelling arrangements for Tuesday; he says he's had an argument with Pat Kenny, our CEO, and we have to get the bus up to Derry on Monday. The boys aren't happy with this. The Gaffer says Kenny told him they had to get on the bus on Monday or "we'll get someone else to take the team up."

"Can we book our own flights on Monday, Gaffer?" Daz Ryan asks.

"No, Daz – everyone on the bus. It'd be crazy otherwise."

Someone asks whether there's any news on the court case.

"I don't know. The Revenue are holding it up but Coughlan has gone underground as far as I can see. I asked Pat Kenny if he could meet me to talk about the travelling but he says he's in a meeting up in Dublin."

We train. Afterwards I'm washing my boots when the Gaffer approaches me.

"You alright, Hogs?"

"Ya, Gaffer. But the uncertainty's getting to me."

"I know," he replies. "It seems Coughlan wants to keep Pat Kenny – that's what he said to me on the phone – but I don't know why."

We're interrupted by an angry, half-naked Joe Gamble coming from the changing rooms out onto the pitch. With a towel around his waist he demands, "What's the f***ing story with the wages, Gaffer? Someone in the club shop says there's none there."

The Gaffer says, "I don't know, Joe."

Gamble angrily reports, "Denis has been on to someone who says they're not in the club shop."

We wander into the changing room. The Gaffer goes off to find out what's going on, at which point Gamble declares, "I'm not f***ing playing tomorrow. That's it."

Kearney takes it upon himself to ring the examiner and try to find out what's happening, without success. He rings the PFAI and explains the situation. Then Jerry Harris, club secretary, says Pat Kenny's in the Cork office alright and not in Dublin as the Gaffer had maintained.

"If he's in the office, what's the Gaffer on about?" Gamble voices what we're all wondering. "Ring the office, Denis."

Denis obliges while everyone looks on. "Ya, he's upstairs in the club shop at a meeting."

A consensus is formed: we should go in there and demand to see him. Get him to tell us what's going on.

Dan Murray, Danny Murphy, Kearney and myself agree to go in.

"Anyone else, lads? Anyone who wants to can come along," says Dan.

Nobody else volunteers.

We decide to meet at 1pm at the office. On the way in I ring ahead and get through to the club shop. Kenny's in a meeting but takes my call and agrees to meet us. When we go in he's in the same meeting room, overlooking Daunt Square, that we met Tynan and then the examiner in.

Meeting with Pat Kenny, CEO of Cork City Football Club

Pat welcomes us in. He says he has no problem talking to us and will start by trying to explain what's gone on since he took over. He tells us we can ask him anything we want.

"When I arrived there were bills coming in left, right and centre. I could have walked away but I said I'd stick it out and try to sort things out. The club was in massive debt – €1 million or so – and in order to try and save it I needed to get us into the examinership process. Reading FC, up to this point, were tracking Dave Mooney; Mathews told me this when I came in. They offered €200,000 and I said no. Then I refused a second offer, so they offered €275,000 and I still said no. Reading started to put me under pressure, and at the time we needed the money for examinership, so I called them and we agreed terms. Mooney was more than happy to get the chance, so the deal was done. The club was saved from liquidation and the examinership process began."

We listen in silence as Kenny continues.

"There was a meeting of creditors last week and they ripped the club apart – and rightly so. They've been owed a lot since before January of this year. But they came onside with 7.5%, so long as they get a percentage of sell-on agreements for Kevin Doyle,

Shane Long and others. The Revenue will get most of the money from these clauses, although they're still not accepting the proposed scheme of arrangement. We should know by next Wednesday or Thursday whether they agree.

"Now, in regard to the possible investors, there were three interested parties but Tom Coughlan was the only one willing to pay money up-front to creditors, and the only one that wanted to keep the club going on a full-time basis."

One of the lads asks, "What about the wages, Pat? That's the reason we came in – we've been told there's no money for our wages."

"Ya, well, we actually had the money for wages earlier in the week, but the problem is that one of the conditions of examinership is that we have to pay bills as they fall due – and a bill came in and we had to pay that first, meaning we then didn't have enough to pay the wages. However, I've just met with Tom Coughlan's accountant and he's going to get the money for the players."

Murph says, quietly, "To be honest with you Pat, if we'd just been told what the situation was there wouldn't have been a problem."

Kearney agrees: "Ya, I suppose it's just a breakdown in communication, but you can see from our side of things that we need to know what's going on."

"You're right, but I didn't want to be stepping on Alan Mathew's toes," says Pat.

Dan Murray asks, "So now we're here we might as well ask you about your plans regarding the budget for the future. Will we be getting the money owed to us?"

Kearney adds, "Ya – we need to get this agreed upfront and on paper."

"No chance," says Kenny. "He [Coughlan] doesn't own the club yet, so we can't get him to sign up for anything. But when he does, make sure to sit him down and talk to him about it."

"How about the travel arrangements to Derry, Pat?' asks Murph. "You know it would give us a better chance if we fly up and have time to rest when we get there."

"At the moment, with the club in examinership, it'd look bad to be seen flying. Therefore you'll have to go by bus."

"The players will understand," says Kearney. "Again, once we know the reason, there's no problem."

Perhaps bolstered by our support, Kenny continues confidently: "And another thing. In future there'll be no more bonuses. Some of the bonuses in lads' contracts are crazy."

We see his point and offer the example of Denis Behan's 'clean sheet' bonus.

Kenny tells us that before we entered examinership €30,000 per week was supposed to be going to the full-time playing staff, with about €25,000 going to the players. From now on it'll be €18,000 a week. (I'm not sure whether this €18,000 only covers players or whether it includes playing staff, but I don't interrupt.)

He then, half-critically, brings up the mind-set of the players for the Galway game, but Dan Murray interrupts him: "It's very difficult for the players at the moment. It might be hard for you to realise just how difficult it is."

But we leave on good terms. The boys are just happy to know what's going on.

~

My 82-year-old grandmother, Anne, rings me later. She always seems to keep an eye on things and is very critical of our performances – although she has a soft spot for Gamble as he's always getting sent off ('my fella', she calls him, even though I'm her grandson).

Tonight she tells me, "I heard on the news that you're all sorted, that that man has taken over the club."

Later we all get a text from the Gaffer saying the wages are to be paid tomorrow by Tom Coughlan.

Friday 10th October

This morning's papers are all on about Drogheda United's problems. Although they won the League last year, and have a huge full-time squad, they're planning to go part time next year. Before the match the lads discuss the prospect of the entire league collapsing.

At any rate we're down to the bare bones again; on the bench we have three reserves who've never trained with the first team.

Dan Murray announces that we should all collect our money, after the match, from an office in the portable cabin outside the dressing rooms.

The floodlights fail five minutes into the warm-up and both teams have to complete it in the dark.

"Nothing going right at this club," someone mutters.

My grandmother's favourite, Joey Gamble, is captain tonight as Dan Murray's suspended. In the team huddle before the game he tells us we have to forget about everything that's going on around us; we have to look out for ourselves and make sure we perform.

"There'll be no sympathy if you play crap," he warns.

The rain's bucketing down and only our hardcore fans are present. But I love these conditions: a slight wind and a greasy surface. We start well and look semi-decent. Lawrie scores a good goal and we're one up at the break.

In my opinion the Gaffer and Biscuits are overly critical of us at half time; players don't need any added negativity at the moment. We're winning 1–0, with only half of our regular players, against a team scrapping for their lives to stay in the division – but the Gaffer's unhappy with a few things and he lets us know. Biscuits is shouting at us to be "more snappy... up for it... brighter!"

In the second half we play badly. Daz Ryan – who was having a decent game up until half time – has a bad few minutes. At one point he has a clearance blocked and, following the resulting throw-in, a harsh penalty awarded against him for handball in the box. I feel sorry for him: he'll bear the brunt of the Gaffer's ire even though the rest of us aren't playing collectively (which is why we're under pressure in the first place).

Everyone's at each other's throats. The match ends and we barrel back into the dressing room.

League of Ireland: Turner's Cross, Cork
Cork City 1–1 Finn Harps

The Gaffer's particularly harsh. He goes through the team and gives out to everyone individually – except for Sully, Nults and myself, who he says did "OK".

Biscuits (who's a postman in his day job) then makes an impromptu speech about it being the worst performance he's seen since he's been at the club. He says we're lucky to be professional footballers, and that no one else will take us at the end of the year.

"Try getting up at six or seven in the morning and ye'll know all about it."

He asks whether fellas are looking after themselves outside of training. I'm not sure where he's coming from. I've always admired Biscuits – and it's likely the Gaffer has given him the job of being bad cop these last few weeks – but tonight, after what the Gaffer already said, there's no need for any more.

We collect our wages afterwards from the portable cabin. It's up to 55% of what we're due for this fortnight.

Later I text Daz Ryan. He's pissed off with football. I tell him he's been our best player for the last month or so (which is true) and he's glad to hear it. We've all been where he is – it's hard to face teammates, the manager, even your family. For Darragh this is all over the smallest of things: the ball, taking an unusual spin, bounced up and hit his hand.

Monday 13th October

We leave from the Silversprings Hotel at midday but we won't get to Derry until around 9pm. It's a gruelling journey, but at least tonight we'll get a tasty meal on arrival.

A few hours into the journey, Danny Murphy, on his way to the toilet at the back of bus, passes me and slaps the broadsheet paper from my hands.

"Sh** paper – no tits!"

Now that he's got my attention he says, "I heard Woodsy's retired. Were you talking to him, Hogs?"

"Lordy mentioned something alright during training, but I wasn't talking to him, no."

"It's true – he's definitely gone," says Murph with resignation.

Come to think of it, against Finn Harps the Gaffer brought two young players on before him, and I remember he did seem a little down in the dressing room afterwards, but he'd said nothing.

I'm saddened that he's gone – almost without anyone noticing.

Tuesday 14th October

We train at 11am this morning for this evening's match, which is unusual for Mathews. It's freezing too, but proves worthwhile when Danny Murphy is nearly dismembered by a ball to the groin during a game of circle. I've never seen a ball deflect so unusually; he falls like a sack of spuds and just lies there on the ground. Most of the players bend double, laughing in the rain and cold, as the steam rises slowly from us into Derry's morning air.

During the match I feel confident on the ball. My touch is good and I'm focused on the game. Young Timmy Kiely finally steps up to the mark and scores a bullet header in the first half, following a particularly crazy run and cross by centre-back (and captain) Dan Murray. Dan's one of those players who seems to be underrated by all except those who've played with him; apart from his outstanding leadership skills, he's got great feet for a centre-back and is always the best player to have in your five-a-side team at training because he's also got an eye for a goal. And tonight, in our hour of need, he's played the captain's role by running the length of the pitch with the ball and crossing for Timmy to score.

Tonight we're all aware that the club's future could actually depend on this result.

In the second half we're under serious pressure and hanging on for our lives; they're sending their whole team into the box and pounding the ball in on top of us. The crowd's roaring, hungry for our blood. But no matter what we do, we can't get out of our own half. We come under avalanche after avalanche of attack, the ball arrowing into our box every few seconds.

Attack the ball, block shots, don't dive in, organise those around you... all these things take place at once. You don't notice time passing; you're fixed in the moment. It's all hands on deck. Everyone's fighting to stay alive, for us as a team – perhaps as a club – to stay alive. People are throwing their bodies in front of shots, hunting every inch for the ball, shouting on teammates, "This is it! Hold on! Just f***ing hold on!"

We have a few hairy moments. Late, late on, their striker Mark Farren makes a run from my position across and behind our centre-half Pat Sullivan, who's playing inside me. One of their players, Higgins, is on the ball near the centre of the pitch and steers a beautifully flighted pass just over Sully's head and in front of the onrushing Farren.

I should go with him – he's run from my area. But I react to his run a split second too late and I'm now a foot behind him, too far to make any impact if he doesn't slow up. "Oh f***," I'm thinking. Sully comes around and both of us are within striking distance for a tackle. But the ball's at his feet – if he shoots now we're dead in the water.

Next thing, our keeper, Mark McNulty, comes out of nowhere and runs into the ball and then into Farren – only just in that order. Farren goes down. The crowd's in uproar. Everyone looks to the ref...

This time last month we were one-up against Derry and it was the last kick of the FAI cup game at the Cross. Farren made the same run and the same ball was played. Mick Devine came out, the ball ran past him and Farren and Mick collided. Outcome: penalty and a draw, followed by a replay in Derry where they beat us on penalties after extra time.

On a scale of one to ten (one being a clear no-penalty and ten being a 'he-did-everything-but-shoot-him'/stonewall penalty) the first incident last month was probably a six, and the ref gave it without hesitation. Right now I'd say this one's a five – a 50/50 collision – but with the home support influencing the ref I'd notch it up to a six, or maybe a seven.

I make out I'm helping Sully clear the ball from the resulting debris, but I eye the ref the whole time. *Don't blow the whistle – don't blow it! Don't lift your hand and point to the spot...*

With a flick of the arm he waves play on and the crisis is over.

Get on with the next ball, the next threat.

I've learned never to ask the ref what's left on the clock at times like this. It helps to keep me focused. Whatever he says – whether it's ten minutes or just one – it seems to distract me into thinking about the result of the match, as if it's already over, rather than what I should be thinking about: the here and now; the ball arriving into our box at pace; whether or not to attack it; the men around me, who are travelling at breakneck speed and will do anything they can to steal the ball away from me, from us... the b*****ds.

The end is clearly nigh when their keeper runs into our box for a corner in a desperate attempt at a glorious equaliser. I'm now hoping I've missed the announcer saying how much time's left, and that we might already be into injury time. *Mustn't think about that now: just pick up a man, stay in your region of the pitch if possible, and if you get the ball punt it long and hard, as far as you can, up the pitch.*

A few minutes later the ref stands in the middle of the pitch, raises his arm to the sky and blows a long, shrill whistle.

Setanta Cup semi-final: The Brandywell, Derry
Derry City 0–1 Cork City

There's elation in the dressing room afterwards – lots of hugging and shouting. Our groundsman, Jerry Kelly, is with us and it seems like he's having the best day of his life. I've never, ever seen him so happy. He cuts a distinctive figure in the dressing room with his beard and substantial beer-belly, hugging and kissing the lads.

I've always felt there's more elation in winning cup semi-finals than even winning the final. There's so much to look forward to: the build-up, the excitement. After a cup final, even when you win, the show's over. Tonight, on the long bus journey home, we can look forward to it all.

Wednesday 15th October

I go to watch the Ireland senior team fixture in Dublin. Two ex-Cork players – Damien Delaney and Shane Long – play well.

Thursday 16th October

A few of us are in the gym this morning when the radio tells us that the High Court hearing in regard to examinership might be deferred for two weeks.

Sean Kelly shouts out, while trying to do a bench press, "For f***'s sake! I can't believe we'll be waiting again!"

Then the Gaffer calls us in for a meeting.

The boys tease Timmy: "You saved the club!"

Timmy giggles.

"You probably did save the club alright, Timmy," I say to him as he sits next to me, "so now might be a good time for contract talks..."

Timmy smiles but says nothing.

"Is everyone here?" the Gaffer asks.

Mick points out that Crazy Daz is missing.

The Gaffer says, "That's OK – he told me he'll be late today. He's cycling in as he hasn't got a car anymore."

He continues, "So. First thing, Muzza heard you're not getting paid the money you're owed. Well, Tom Coughlan rang me and it's not true – he'll be paying you your money. And he's still obliged to pay you, so that hasn't changed."

We ask him about the possible court delay that was announced the radio; the Gaffer says he hasn't heard about it, and that it would be a disaster if true.

"Anyway," he continues, "I was talking to Coughlan yesterday about the final. I want to do it right, to treat it properly. I asked him about suits and he said kinda ya, kinda no. How much were your suits for the FAI Cup final last year?"

Dan Murray answers, half-speculatively, "About two or three hundred euro, Gaffer, I'd say."

"Well that's a bit pricey alright. How many of you have suits from last year?"

Most hands go up.

"So only about three or four of you don't. So let's get shirts and ties for everyone and suits for those few, OK? And if there's any problem with your old suits just wear a different one – there's no bother there. Now, do you want to stay in a hotel before the final?"

The boys are quiet.

Dan answers, "I don't know, Gaffer."

Denis says the same.

Gamble chips in, "To be honest, if it's in Cork I'd prefer to stay in my own house."

Decision made.

"OK. And how about training the morning of the match, like we did in Derry, and then going to a hotel afterwards for sleep and pre-match?"

The lads are silent again.

"I'm not trying to force this on you, lads – just tell me whether you want it or not."

We say no; we'd prefer just to treat it like a normal league game and have training the night before.

"Do you know how many tickets we're going to get?" Dan asks.

The Gaffer responds, "How many did yee get for FAI cup?"

"Four each."

"I'll talk to him about it later. And just in regard to revenue from the gates, lads, the breakdown will be 40% to us, 40% to Derry, and 20% going to the FAI for the game costs."

The Gaffer continues, "Coughlan's also on about advertising the final; he says he'll try to get all the lads who've recently moved across the channel from here to help out. So that's Flynny, Mooney, Doyler, Shane Long... who else is there?"

The lads help him out with more names, including Alan Bennett, Roy O'Donovan, David Meyler, Damien Delaney, Brian Barry-Murphy and Leon McSweeney.

"He's going to get them to do ads for the radio here. Apparently Seán Óg Ó hAilpín is being asked too, as well as some Munster rugby players."

I interrupt, "Ah, Gaffer, you'll have to get Denis to do one!"

Cue Mark Nulty: "*Ah geeeeba Jesus... come to the match fellas... ah holy God!*"

The lads enjoy this, including Denis, who declares, "Ah, I'd be happy to do one Gaffer – not a bother," and sits back, smiling.

The Gaffer quietens us down with a hand gesture before continuing.

"Seriously, though. We need to win the match, boys. I'm telling you – Glentoran are a good side. They're top of their league up North and they have some very dangerous players – particularly Gary Hamilton, who, as I'm sure you'll know, is an international. They beat Derry, Pat's and Drogheda to get here, so don't take them lightly."

The lads are up for it; the anticipation's palpable.

"Now one last thing. Remember that golf day I promised you for achieving the goals we'd set? Well I've sorted it: I'm bringing you to Kenmare. Didn't think I'd sort that, did yee?" he says, laughing.

The boys' eyes light up, and Mick Devine (who loves golf) almost jumps out of his seat.

"We'll go up by bus Wednesday and come back Thursday."

Our club doctor, Ger Murphy, walks into the room. The lads give him some light-hearted abuse. He's a top bloke, and has been coming in unpaid these last few weeks. The lads are genuinely happy to see him.

"Nice to finally see you, Doc," says Mick, who is still hysterical about the golfing news.

"I'm only here for the money," the Doc answers, laughing.

The Gaffer ends the meeting with talk of tomorrow's match against Drogheda.

"Their heads will be down, boys [due to their club's financial issues]. We know what it's like – it's a s*** situation. The guy that was our examiner is moving onto them.

"But let's go and win. They're likely to have ten points deducted, so we've got a chance of finishing in fourth and getting a shout in Europe. It'd be s*** to see Sligo take it away from us. Let's finish the season on a high."

We leave the dressing room happier than we've been for ages.

During warm-up I catch a volley right on the money and try to knock it back across the pitch, but I catch Timmy – who's looking the other way – on the head with it.

I apologise, feeling bad.

"No bother, Hog," he says, after regaining his composure.

The boys laugh at him, which makes me feel even worse.

"Just remember: you saved the club," I tell him, but there's no smile from him this time.

I start to feel tired and cranky. Denis and Sully pull out of training with minor nicks and I almost decide to follow them in, but then I tell myself to get something out of it, and before I know it training's over.

Getting changed in the dressing room, Kearney announces that he's got a missed call from Stephen McGuinness. Something might be up. He rings him back, chats briefly and hangs up.

"Alright lads: it's sorted. Coughlan owns the club."

Friday 17th October

from the *Irish Examiner*, 17th October 2008:

CORK CITY FC: GREEN LIGHT FOR NEW OWNER

Property developer Tom Coughlan has been given the go-ahead by the High Court to take over ownership of Cork City Football Club.

A delighted Mr Coughlan officially took the reins yesterday after Mr Justice Peter Kelly ruled in favour of his bid to take over the club, ending the constraints of examinership under which the club has been operating since August. He was installed as the new owner after the court approved a deal reached with creditors of the Eircom Premier Division club.

"I am greatly looking forward to the challenge," said Mr Coughlan, a 40-year-old Douglas-based property developer and hotelier. "In these difficult economic circumstances, it is important for the people of Cork to support our only national soccer club. Our

immediate focus will, of course, be on the Setanta Sports Cup in two weeks' time and we will be trying to end the season on a successful note."

A financial scheme aimed at ensuring the survival of the club was approved in the Commercial Court. It follows a two-month period in which the owners, Cork City Investment FC Ltd, have been under the protection of the court after the appointment of Kieran McCarthy of Hughes Blake Chartered Accountants as examiner.

Previously, the court heard, Cork City owed its creditors €1.3 million, including €360,000 to the Revenue Commissioners. A number of players and staff had to be let go and the fortnightly wages bill had been reduced from €91,000 to €71,000.

Yesterday, the court heard that investor Tom Coughlan has committed significant funding to the club, while a survival scheme in which creditors will receive a percentage of the money owed to them had been drawn up by the examiner. The only creditor to oppose the scheme was the Revenue Commissioners,

whose objections Mr Justice Kelly described as not
having any validity. Club manager Alan Mathews will
now seek a meeting with Mr Coughlan as players and
staff enter their sixth week of pay cuts.

~

Before the game the Drogheda players talk to us like
never before, complimenting us on how we've kept
winning despite everything. However, the match is a
dull affair.

League of Ireland: Turner's Cross, Cork
Cork City 1–1 Drogheda United

Sunday 19th October

Today *The Sunday Times* newspaper featured a piece
entitled "Arkaga Head Man In Fraudulent Car Sales."
The article explains how during a High Court action in
England in 1997, Gerard Walsh's evidence was
"rejected by the presiding judge who reached a

finding of 'fraudulent misrepresentation' against the businessman.'' The Court then awarded £677,000 (€873,000) damages for deceit against Walsh.

The article also covered the FAI's reaction...

from the *Sunday Times*, 19th October 2008:

John Delaney, chief executive of the FAI, claimed that Arkaga had reneged on a commitment to the FAI that it would continue funding Cork City until the end of the season. Branding the company a disgrace, Delaney said it had let down the club, players, staff and supporters. At recent home games, fans voiced their anger at both Walsh and Arkaga. One banner unfurled during a match against Bray Wanderers read: "Arkaga – rot in hell".

Wednesday 23rd October

We're in Kenmare on the trip the Gaffer organised as a reward for reaching goals set by him earlier in the season. A day of golf, followed by dinner and drinks:

fantastic. Days (and nights) out like this are rare. There's no match at the weekend and we have a week and a half until our next game so it's an ideal time to give the lads some relief from all the recent chaos.

I survive the golf (but only barely, as Dan Murray almost kills me with a drive just passed my head). I don't like golf but most of the lads love it; Mick Devine is positively ecstatic, strutting around the course in splendid golfing attire.

Afterwards, back at the hotel, the Gaffer calls a meeting as he says Tom Coughlan wants to speak to us all. We gather in a meeting room and the Gaffer and Tom sit at opposite ends.

Tom starts by outlining his plans. He talks about the club needing to do more community work; he suggests giving players extra jobs within the club to help it become a more sustainable outfit.

Throughout this the Gaffer's body language is not good, and Tom doesn't seem to be registering anything he's saying with him.

When Tom finishes, someone asks, "How about the €15,000 budget – is that true?"

Healers adds, "Ya, and could I just ask – do you want to win the league next year or would you settle for fifth place or something like that?"

Tom replies without flinching: "What do you think, Colin?"

Healers bats back: "I don't know – I'm asking you."

Tom: "What do you think?"

Healers (more aggressively): "I said I'm asking you."

Tom (equally aggressively): "Yes, Colin, but what do you *think*?"

Healers doesn't back down: "I'm asking you."

Tom finally obliges: "*Of course* I want to win the league!"

Denis changes the subject by saying something daft, and raises a laugh.

Then Kearney asks about contracts and, still without looking at Mathews, Tom says he has a meeting with the Gaffer on Friday and will see about the rest of us after that. He then says he wants to sign players from the UK who aren't getting first-team football at the moment – players like Colin Doyle and Alan Bennett.

I wonder, if he's the one deciding who to sign, where this leaves the Gaffer.

After the meeting the players go off as a group to have a meal. The nuances of Tom Coughlan's answers, and the Gaffer's body language, are recounted in great detail.

We all agree that the Gaffer's under threat. It seems further cutbacks are also likely, but at least Coughlan's met us – unlike Gerard Walsh. So we'll wait and see. And at least we'll be getting paid 100% of our wages this Friday.

After dinner we have a few drinks and Denis gives a superb rendition of *Rattlin' Bog* in a previously sleepy Kenmare pub.

Thursday 23rd October

The long bus trip home is made painfully longer when we get caught in a flash flood in the Kenmare mountains, but the lads are in good spirits after the night out.

On finally arriving home we get a text from Éanna: *Message from Alan – bikes taken from hotel last night. Need to be returned. Where are they? Please call Alan.*

(The hotel that we stayed in had offered complementary bicycles, and some of the lads thought it a good idea to cycle them around the place in the dark. The gaffer won't be impressed.)

Friday 24th October

The Gaffer calls a meeting out on the pitch.

"First things first: some bikes went missing from the hotel the other night. Now let's get this sorted. Where are they? I saw you wheeling past me in the middle of night, Denis, and there was only one bike outside the hotel this morning..."

Denis is indignant: "That was my bike that was outside the hotel when we left."

"Was that the one you were on when you flew by me in the middle of night?"

"Yes – that was it, Gaffer."

"Then where are the other two bikes, lads? There are three bikes missing." The Gaffer's getting agitated.

But Denis seems surprised: "Three bikes, Gaffer?"

"Yes. There were three bikes taken and we need to get them back."

Denis thinks about it for a few seconds before replying, "Gaffer I had a bike, there might have been someone else on another bike but I definitely didn't see a third bike – honestly."

The Gaffer takes a deep breath and looks seriously at Denis.

Gamble enters the fray, backing Denis's story up: "He's right, Gaffer, there were two taken – definitely not three."

"Where's the second one, then?"

"It's probably back at the hotel too, Gaffer," suggests Gamble.

"OK, well just make sure someone contacts the hotel to let them know where the bikes are – whether there are two of them or just one. OK?"

Denis agrees to contact the hotel later on.

Then Seany clears his throat and announces, "Also, Gaffer, I have set of golf clubs to give back to the golf club. They're rentals but I didn't get a chance to give them back. They're in the boot of my car."

The Gaffer's wearing an expression of pure disbelief.

He inhales deeply. "Well you'd better hand them back when you go home then, Seany" (Seany's from Tralee).

He takes another deep breath: "F***ing hell, lads! Right – let's get on with training, shall we? We have to concentrate on the final from here on in. No more distractions; good behaviour all the way. I'll get Glentoran watched, too."

In training, predictably, he runs us to death. At the end we have a long game and he screams at us throughout. He picks Denis out for extra work, and Denis really suffers – but then walks into the dressing room afterwards smiling about the bikes. In fact we all feel good afterwards, and are happy enough to be ordered into the pre-prepared ice baths.

Later I'm asked by a guy who's doing work experience in the club office if I could give him a lift into town. I tell him no problem, but as soon as he gets into my car he starts giving me a hard time.

"Are yee going to beat Glentoran, then?"

"Hopefully, yes."

"But they're crap, aren't they?"

"No. They beat Derry, Pat's and Drogheda to get here; they're definitely not crap."

"What do you think of Mathews?"

"He's very good, very organised…"

The guy interrupts: "Better than Rico, or than Dolan?"

"No, just different. Rico was good too – and so was Dolan. He was…"

He interrupts again: "How about Farrelly?"

"He's a great player."

"But why did he leave?"

"He didn't leave – he got sick."

"But why hasn't he come back?"

It goes on like this, unrelenting, for the entire journey.

Later I finally ring Woodsy. He says he half regrets not holding on until the end of the season but couldn't hack the bench, which I understand. But after all he's done for the club it would've been nice to see him get a send-off of some kind.

Chapter Ten

25th October to End of Season 2008

Saturday 25th October

A week to go until the cup final and we're back to 100% of our wages. Brilliant. We're all delighted. The Gaffer's up north watching Glentoran so Biscuits takes training, which means old-school running for 40 minutes, followed by a game.

Monday 27th October

I arrive early, and as usual Mick and Dan Murray are early too. Mick's warming his hands through his goalkeeper gloves on an industrial heater that he's dragged into the dressing room when Crazy Daz (just back from last week's Ireland under-23s call-up) walks into the room fully kitted out in Ireland tracksuit, complete with Umbro hat and gloves.

"For f***'s sake, Daz – you don't have to wear the whole gear," says Mick.

Daz is not discouraged; he has the same broad, crazy grin on his face as usual. "Better than Denis's gear," he decides, and the lads laugh.

During training it comes to our attention that Tom Coughlan is in the stand, watching.

Tuesday 28th October

Today I ring the firm of solicitors about starting my apprenticeship next year. I can feel it's time to get it done.

At training the lads are chatting about a piece in the *Echo* last night. It said there'd be a budget of about €15,000 for the playing wages this year. It also said players would leave if this was the case.

We wonder who might've spoken to the reporter but nobody owns up. I don't want to think about that at all today – I just want to gear up for Saturday's final.

While I'm washing my boots afterwards I get chatting to Jerry Kelly, who as usual is armed with a shovel.

"What do you think of the latest events?" he asks.

"I'm trying to keep my mind off it all, Jerry – I just want to focus on the match. But I'm not particularly happy with these rumours going around about the future of the club, the cutbacks etc."

"It looks like we've gone from the frying pan into the fire," he tells me, and starts shovelling sand from a wheelbarrow onto the pitch. "There'll only be Éanna and Laura [the office lady] left at the club, the way things are going."

I go into the gym. Gamble follows me in; I suspect he'll be doing some seriously tough and technical workout, so to save my embarrassment I decide to leave.

"Just win game on Saturday. Forget everything else, eh Joe?"

"That's it Hog – just win the game."

I go shower.

The Gaffer picks myself, Danny Murphy, Crazy Daz and Denis to go to the cup-final press conference at Beamish and Crawford's showroom. Members of the local and national media are present when we arrive.

The Gaffer does all the early talking, answering questions about Glentoran, the current situation at the club and rumours surrounding it. Each of the players is then interviewed, but it's child's play compared to the work experience guy in my car last week.

There's a buzz beginning to grow about the city – I can feel it. Everyone's talking about the match. It's important to use this attention in the right way in order to remain focused on the playing side of the game.

I text Kearney, who's injured. He says his leg's getting better and he's hoping it'll be good for Saturday. He's concerned that he might have to look for another club during the off-season.

The situation's unsettling for everyone, but we just need to try and concentrate on Saturday's match until then.

Thursday 30th October

We received a group text from Éanna yesterday saying he has all our tickets for the final and we should just go and ask him for them. I appreciate it: the last thing we need is ticket issues on the day before the game. I went to see him and gave him €200 for ten tickets, and everyone's looking for more.

This morning we're training in the cold. The lads are wearing gloves and hats, and Crazy Daz is still sporting his Umbro Ireland kit.

I'm standing on the outside of a playing grid when Biscuits says to me, "The boys are looking sharp today."

Biscuits is a great reader of the game so I'm glad to hear him saying that. We'll need to be sharp. Glentoran will be sharper than us match-wise as they've had regular games the last few weeks, whereas we haven't played for two weeks, and rustiness can creep in... We had a distracting two-week gap before the 2005 FAI cup-final defeat, and I've always thought rustiness played some part in our undoing that day.

Today we play games, 3 v 3 and 4 v 4, and the boys are happy with it. You can tell things are gearing up nicely.

Afterwards there's another impromptu meeting; the Gaffer's there with Tom Coughlan and both are looking agitated.

Nulty whispers to me, "Tom's fuming – wait and see."

Tom paces up and down at the head of the room while we take our seats and anticipate a tongue-lashing. He goes into a tirade about our 'behaviour' in Kenmare. He found out today that someone had been climbing a wardrobe in their hotel room and broke it. He's had to pay for it. He also says guests in another room were kept up all night and the hotel had to reimburse them, and he's paid for that too.

"I thought about letting it go until after the final, but then I decided against it. This kind of stuff is not acceptable on my watch."

The players keep quiet. We can see his side of things and it's fair enough.

Afterwards, on the way out, the Gaffer asks me, "Did we let ourselves down, do you think?"

"No, Gaffer. We were just letting off steam. It's been a long year. If that's the worst we've done I'll take it; we can just concentrate on the cup final now."

He gives me a DVD of Glentoran in the semi-final, which I'd asked for, and we leave.

I'll need to get rid of my tickets tonight – the cup final's only two days away.

Friday 31st October

It's our last training session before the final and I'm concentrating on the small things. I'm wearing long studs for a change: due to the recent weather I'll probably need to wear them for the final.

We watch video clips of Glentoran afterwards. The Gaffer talks about one of their better players – centre-forward Gary Hamilton. He tells Murph this guy has good movement and that he can crop up anywhere.

Their keeper likes to find him directly to his feet, out wide. Murph and myself need to cut this out.

"But we can't lose our own shape. Set pieces too – he takes most of them. Whips it in near-post. He's a good player, lads."

He tells us where he thinks we can get at them.

Saturday 1st November

I can already sense the atmosphere when I park up at the ground a good two-and-a-half hours before kick-off. I wish it was like this every week, crowds swarming all over the place.

However, on arriving into the ground at 5.30pm Dan Murray informs us that our usual pre-match tea and toast at the Turner's Cross Tavern has been called off. There's been trouble up there between the fans and the owner's been hurt. So we have to wait at the ground for an hour-and-a-half before the Gaffer's talk.

There are a few surprises on the team-sheet when the Gaffer announces it: Mick Devine's left out; Nulty's in; Darragh Ryan's out and Kearney's in.

Usual up front; Alan O'Connor on the left; and Timmy joins Lordy, who's half-injured, on the bench.

The Gaffer makes a speech about getting the things in life that you want, about working hard to get them. He tells us we've worked hard all year and this could be our reward; that we deserve it after all we've been through, but that we have to perform to our best in order to win it.

We're jittery in the first half, as if the crowd has got to us. Their lad Hamilton back-heels the ball through my legs and gets big cheer from the travelling contingent of Glentoran fans.

They score soon after.

They seem to be winning 50/50s; we're barking at each other and panicking. I'm thinking it could be one of those days when nothing goes right, but I'm also fighting that thought.

At half time Gamble takes the impetus: "We just need a bit more composure, lads. This might be the last time we play together – don't be shouting at each

other if someone makes a mistake. We seem panicky –
we just need to calm down."

Dan Murray says, "Come on lads, for f***'s sake.
We've come all this way. Don't f*** it up now."

The Gaffer advises, "Don't let it behind ye, lads –
especially by not performing. Go out there second half
and up the ante. Get at them, for Christ's sake, and I
promise ye, yee'll win."

Kearney, coming out of the toilet, loses it
completely: "Come on lads, for f***'s sake! We're
not losing this f***ing match! We just need to have
the balls to go at them. It's f***ing there for us –
come on, for f***'s sake!" His voice has gone high-
pitched and some of the lads start laughing. Crazy
Daz, giggling, tells him to calm down.

The lads are amused, but Kearney's approach
seems to work: if he's not afraid to make a fool out of
himself in front of us, then maybe we can do the same
outside. At least that's how I'm feeling.

We go out second half and tear into them. The crowd's all behind us now, too. Getting the ball down my side and attacking the Shed End is a real thrill.

The Hamilton situation is sorted too, as Alan O'Connor (who's moved to my wing) is reading it better and cutting it off. All the running we've done lately is paying off; our fitness is really showing. Every one of our players is coming to the fore, getting a real grip on the game.

Then we score: Dan Murray with a header from a corner. As our boys celebrate I watch the heads of the Glentoran players drop. They know they're in trouble now.

Not much later Kearney – the little man, so often the scorer of important goals – scores our second with a great ball from Alan O'Connor and a header from Denis setting it up.

We have a few scrappy moments but we hang on.

The celebrations afterwards are great; recent difficulties seem to melt away for a moment. The exaltation of victory in a cup final at the Cross fills our minds and hearts for one night at least.

Setanta cup final, Turner's Cross, Cork
Cork City 2–1 Glentoran

Monday 3rd November

When I arrive at the ground Jerry Kelly's singing *"All-Ireland champions, All-Ireland Champions"* whilst mopping up in the corridor. Everyone's in great form. The lads are winding Kearney up as he cried in a TV interview after the game; they're also taking the piss out of Crazy Daz for not being able to get into Havana Browns nightclub on Saturday night because of his dodgy clobber, and for cursing on TV. He said something like, "Ya, its f***ing great," and a studio presenter had to apologise for him.

We have to play St Pat's tomorrow in Dublin – we still have a chance of getting into Europe (thanks to Drogheda's plight) but Sligo are catching us.

In training we have small-sided games and the lads are a bit tired and narky. Afterwards we talk about contracts: there's only a week left of the season and we're all wondering what's going on. The cup final was fantastic, but now we're back to reality with a bang. Our attention has returned to the anticipated cutbacks and the money we're owed.

Tuesday 4th November

On the bus to Dublin, Daz Ryan and myself discuss our options, should things go pear-shaped. He has a buddy in Melbourne who's playing in the part-time league below the A-league.

"The money's only OK, but the lifestyle's great," he says.

It sounds nice, but we'll wait and see. Everything's so uncertain here. Money's still owed to us and the likelihood of getting it back is decreasing by the day. Coughlan has to pay everyone who's owed money, including players no longer involved in the squad. Some think there's a strong possibility he'll try to negotiate downwards the amount owed to people whose contracts are up, in exchange for the offer of a new contract.

Denis is on about PFAI rep McGuinness coming down tomorrow, but Gamble doesn't think he's coming down.

"We need to ask him to come down to talk for us," says Daz Ryan, "otherwise it could get personal – and that won't be good for anyone."

We get to Richmond Park, home of St. Pat's. It's freezing and we find it hard to motivate ourselves. Kearney and Gamble are getting abuse from St Pat's fans during the warm-up; the crowd's sparse and the comments are easily heard. It's not nice, but as they say, such abuse is really a compliment.

In the first half of the match we knock the ball around confidently and, despite Pat's having a strong team out, we dominate. Muzza makes sure everyone's putting it in.

The whistle goes for half time. Sometimes I hate half time, with the thought of another 45 minutes to go. I try to get myself to stop thinking. I change my boots as the pitch is chopping up.

In the second half I make a few mistakes but get away with them. Denis does well to win a free at the edge of their area; Danny Murphy puts it low and to the left side of the wall and it goes in.

Murph goes nuts – he hasn't scored since 2004.

League of Ireland: Richmond Park, Inchicore, Dublin
St. Patrick's Athletic 0–1 Cork City

On the way off the pitch we clap our 100 or so fans, and I hear "Well done, Hoggie!" from somewhere high above me in stand. It's Tom Coughlan.

"Cheers Tom," I mouth, and go in.

Friday 7th November

It's been absolutely lashing for the last 48 hours and now it's dull and cold too. The Gaffer's initially in good form, but then he switches to serious mode.

"Win tonight, boys, and that's your work done for the season. If we go about it properly we'll get the victory."

It's raining hard during the warm-up and we come into the dressing room drenched. There's a crowd of about 2,500 but I don't blame people for not showing up in this weather.

The first half's a scrappy affair, the second similar, and the game ends in a draw. It's a fair result.

League of Ireland: Turner's Cross, Cork
Cork City 0–0 Sligo Rovers

The Gaffer's not happy afterwards and gives out to strikers for lack of movement.

"You weren't at the races tonight, boys. Just not good enough. You've *got* to put in a good week's work next week."

I say to Muzza, who's sitting next to me, "We never do it the easy way, do we?"

"No, that's not the Cork City way – recently at least," he replies.

Monday 10th November

This morning the Munster rugby team are training in 'the Farm' area of Bishopstown as I drive past. We've been driving past them all year; they always have big flashy vans full of training gear and refreshments for their players and their ten or so coaches.

I look across to our own area of the ground as I'm driving and see the Gaffer putting cones out by himself.

Munster are playing the All-Blacks next week in their new 25,000-seater stadium. To my right as I drive is the new greyhound track – another state-of-the-art facility. Bishopstown, on the other hand, is in a shoddy state of disrepair and is looking particularly cold and dreary this morning.

A lot of players are injured and there's no sign of 'No-Show Joe' or Lawrie. Later the Gaffer calls us into a meeting room.

"I want to put yee in the know lads – let yee know what my dealings with him were, what the situation is."

The boys listen intently.

"I met with Tom Coughlan last Thursday for three hours. He asked me to take a 65% wage cut and I told him I wouldn't do that. I understand he's planning to do the same with the players, but I told him it wouldn't work out. He says it's unsustainable to continue as we are, that cuts are necessary. I asked him why he got involved if he didn't have the money to keep it going; he said he wanted to do it for the community, to build the club, etc.

"He said there are other ways of paying players, such as giving them free rent on a house or something – like they do in England and Dublin, and like they used to in this league. I told him the Cork players would leave if presented with the kind of cuts he has in mind, but he seems to think there'd be nowhere for you to go, as other clubs are in the s*** also. I told him he's a fool to think you don't have other options.

"He does think of some of you as brands, though. Muzza – he sees you as a brand, and Kearney and Healy. Even you, Hogs."

"You're definitely Lidl, Hogs. And Muzza's Tesco," Denis announces.

Mick Devine chips in: "And you're Michael Guineys, Denis!"

The lads are sniggering away at this when Kearney interrupts, cold as ice: "People here definitely have other options, Gaffer. The only problem is that we can't go anywhere in Ireland until January."

Murph adds, "If I was out of contract now I'd be looking for another club. But what about the money that's owed to us? When's he planning to pay that?"

The Gaffer says, "I asked him about that and he said he'll pay it back by the end of November."

Mick D breaks in: "What about signing players, Gaffer? Remember the ones he mentioned in Kenmare? Alan Bennett and Colin Doyle..."

"Ya, I do remember – he thought two Cork lads not playing regularly in England might want to come back."

Someone points out that he also said we've only got a budget of €15,000.

Healy asks, "Where's Doyle playing?"

"Birmingham."

"Oh ya – we'll definitely get him, then," Healy jibes.

The Gaffer agrees: "I know. He's probably on €15,000 a *week* – we'll never get him for a few hundred. Likewise Benno."

Kearney says, "So it's all bulls**t about staying full time with that kind of budget. It'd be better for the lads to know at this stage."

"I know, Liam. That's the way it seems. I still want to keep us together, though, and I told him so. I told him who I want to keep, and that I want to bring in a few more players. We could do well, challenge for things. But it's not fair what's happening to the players at the moment; there's no way in any other job would you be asked to do the same work and the same hours for 65% less than your normal wage. No way."

Kearney says what we're all thinking: "The way it looks now is he's getting us to work our balls off for this European spot, and whether or not we get it he's going to put us all on €300-a-week contracts afterwards."

Muzza breaks in angrily: "I feel like I just want to get the money I'm owed and get the hell out of here."

I feel the same way.

The Gaffer keeps a level head. "I know, but you need to stick together in regard to the money you're owed. I told him I'd compromise on some of the money I'm owed, and that I'd negotiate a percentage drop in my wages on top of that. I also told him I wanted to stay and build on the group that's here. I took a break from my job for three years and I want to finish the job here. My mind hasn't changed on that."

But Muzza doesn't budge: "There's no way we should accept anything less than what we're owed from him."

Murph says, "We should get that promise of his – to pay us back by the end of November – in writing."

The Gaffer wants to know if we've got any more questions.

Someone suggests a meeting with Coughlan; Healy wants to get him in tomorrow.

The Gaffer doesn't comment on this, but he says, "I also asked him about going on from here, getting lads on proper fitness programs for the off-season like professional clubs do."

Muzza asks, "He doesn't want to pay us in the off-season though, does he?"

"I don't know... but I asked him about getting us away for pre-season training like we did this year, told him it cost about €20,000. He eventually suggested that the money he promised yee for winning the Setanta and getting fourth place and into Europe

(€10,000) could be used to pay for it – but that it should be called a holiday."

"Some f***ing holiday," Denis retorts.

The Gaffer says, "Ya. I've got my doubts. He told us in previous meetings that he was buying the pub, and it turns out he hasn't bought it at all. I also heard that he's pissed off with the MFA over an incident in the Shed where the barriers broke, and he's talking about moving to Musgrave Park and an all-purpose stadium. Seems like he's acting erratically to me, and yes – as if he doesn't know what he's doing. He also said Madjeski, the chairman of Reading, rang him after we won the Setanta Cup to congratulate him."

Mick says, "He told me he played golf with Tiger Woods. Honestly – I swear to God."

The lads have a laugh but I'm wondering whether or not to believe Mick.

"And that's not all," he continues, "Princess Diana was in one of the magazines in the office and when he saw it he said he'd danced with her."

Boys laugh nervously, clearly unsure what to believe.

The meeting ends when the Gaffer says it's time to get training, and we wander out, depressed.

There are only eight outfield players, plus three goalies, but we have a good session. I'm on fire in the shooting session – everything comes off. Outside of my right: top corner; inside of my right: drive to top corner; disguised chip… catching it perfectly.

It feels great to be playing well, but others are not hitting the ball so well and there are definitely a few heads down.

Daz Ryan whispers to me during the shooting drill, "There's not really much motivation today, is there Hogs. Probably because we're all going to be unemployed next week..."

There are already rumours of players leaving. Muzza scores a great goal and Nulty shouts, "*Come on St. Johnstone!*"

"Just two days of training left, thank God," says Muzza, who loves a countdown.

Wednesday 12th November

In the changing room this morning the boys discuss
the contract talks and people leaving. I'll be surprised,
judging by these discussions, if we hold onto even half
our team. It seems Tom Coughlan has called the
highest-profile players and offered them low amounts
– some even 50% lower than what they're on at the
moment. Apparently the lads in question (Healy,
Muzza, Kearney) all told him they're not interested in
such contracts. He also called Joe Gamble and told
him he wants to reduce his wages, even though Joe's
in contract for another two years. Joe said he's not up
for that. And why should he be?

After training, while we're still on the pitch, the
Gaffer pulls me aside. He says the amount Tom's
likely to offer me is around 50% of my current
contract, like the other boys. I tell him I wouldn't be
interested in that, but I *would* be willing to take a cut if
the terms were right. In other words, if they allowed

me to start my law course in the last two months of the contract.

The Gaffer approves of this, "So how about something like a 20% cut?"

"Ya, I'd be happy with whatever Kearney's on. Tell Kearney he's my agent – he'll talk a harder game than me."

Later, Kearney rings me to check how much we're now owed. The first referral was 30% of our fortnightly wage, then two weeks later it was 50%, then 55%, then 55% again. We're therefore missing 210% of our gross fortnightly – or 420% of our gross weekly – wage. It'd be great to get that back: we could all do with it.

Thursday 13th November
It's the final training session of the season and Dan Murray and myself are delighted. Gamble, who's suspended for the last two games of the season, comes

in anyway to see whether there's any news about the contracts. He's disappointed to discover there is none.

"No f***ing scandal, for f***'s sake."

"Just keep your phone on tomorrow, Joe," Dan advises.

Friday 14ᵗʰ November

Last trip, thank God. The boys are in good form even though nothing's been sorted. I enjoy the trip because I'm sitting with Daz Ryan. He's a relaxed character; nothing's ever too stressful for him and there's always a glimmer of light somewhere. He says he's definitely moving to Oz and has sent his CV to a few clubs over there. He'd like to stay but he thinks the Gaffer's being cagey with him at the moment. Told him about the budget and said if he can sort 'the lads' he'll see about Daz afterwards, which obviously made Daz feel like an outsider.

Talk returns to tonight's match. If Sligo draw, we're through to Europe no matter what... but that's not likely.

Dan Murray hands out sheets from the PFAI, asking us to work out how much we're owed. Denis is loudest trying to figure it out, and he doesn't make much sense.

I sleep on the bus. It's been a tough season but we're nearly there.

League of Ireland: Dalymount Park, Dublin
Bohemians 3–0 Cork City

We get battered by the league champions, and Sligo win their match. We finish fifth and miss out on Europe. We would have finished fourth and got the European place if we hadn't had those ten points deducted.

As there's no news of contracts, on hearing the final whistle most of us have become unemployed. So the uncertainty continues.

~

Final Standings – League of Ireland - 2008

		Pld	W	D	L	Pts
1.	Bohemians	33	27	4	2	85 CL
2.	St. Patrick's Ath.	33	20	6	7	66 EL
3.	Derry City	33	16	10	7	58 EL
4.	Sligo Rovers	33	12	12	9	48 EL
5.	**Cork City**	**33**	**15**	**11**	**7**	**46***
6.	Bray Wanderers	33	11	6	16	39
7.	Shamrock Rovers	33	8	13	12	37
8.	Drogheda United	33	12	9	12	35*
9.	Galway United	33	8	8	17	32
10.	Finn Harps	33	9	4	20	31 R
11.	Cobh Ramblers	33	6	8	19	19 R
12.	UCD	33	4	9	29	21 R

CL = Qualified for Champions League

EL = Qualified for Europa League

* Deducted ten points on entering examinership

~

Chapter Eleven

*Mathews was fired as CCFC manager in December 2008

Neal Horgan: How did your move to Cork come about?

Alan Mathews: Well, I'd just left Longford Town FC. My contract had ended and I felt it was time to move on. I'd been fortunate to have a very good relationship with the Chairman and all of the board members at the club, and in the end we finished on great terms. I'd been there since 2002, six seasons or so, and I'd really enjoyed it. We had a lot of success: two wins out of four FAI cup final appearances; one win out of two league cup finals; good strong positions in the league; qualification for Europe... great times for the club. But by the end of 2007 I knew it was the end. That year, despite getting to the cup final (which we lost to Cork City), we were relegated. It was a hard blow to take, certainly, in the circumstances.

NH: In what circumstances?

AM: The club had been late filing their paperwork and we were deducted eight points as a result. If we'd had those eight points we would've finished well clear of relegation – nearly mid-table. But we didn't have them and we were relegated.

NH: So how did the Cork job come about?

AM: Well, my last game with Longford was actually the 2007 cup final. It had been delayed – something to do with the fact that the RDS ground was being used for the match, as Lansdowne was under development. In any event, we lost and my spell was over. I didn't want to continue. I told them, and in fairness they wanted me to stay but they understood my decision.

So I just continued working in the bank where I'd been all along anyway.

Then, not long after the cup final, I received a call out of the blue from a man named Denis O'Sullivan. He said he was involved with Arkaga, the owners of Cork City FC, and that he'd like to discuss the possibility of appointing me to the job at Cork. He asked if I'd meet him at Jury's Hotel a few days later. I was working in the IFSC [International Financial Services Centre] just across the road at the time, so I said yes and a few days later crossed the bridge to meet him.

We discussed the matter and I told him I'd be interested, so we agreed to set up another meeting a week later, this time at the Merrion Hotel. On this occasion Aidan Tynan was also present and I told both men I was definitely interested. They told me it would be a full-time position, which is what I wanted as I knew that was the way football here was going at the time.

NH: Full time?

AM: Yes. If you remember, Drogheda had very strong financial backing at the time, as (seemingly) did Bohemians, St. Pat's and – for a few years before this – Shelbourne. All these teams, along with Cork City, had gone full time. It was back in the days of the Celtic Tiger; it seemed an industry was finally being created here – a professional football industry. Attendances were up, full-time players had brought success in Europe... there was a great buzz about the league in general. Alas, we all know what happened next, but at the time it felt like Irish domestic football was on the up and up, and I was as excited as anybody else about it.

After the second meeting I decided to do some research on Arkaga, as they'd told me they were very well capitalised and in a very strong position financially to back the club. I looked into them and discovered they were fund managers – hedge fund managers. But their info checked out and they seemed in a very healthy position, financially.

NH: So you took the job?

AM: I met them again about the 18th or 19th of December. This time Gerard Walsh was present. It was very clear that Mr Walsh was the main man; he projected himself as such. He asked about coaching and what qualifications I held. I found this strange, to be honest. Anyway I told him I had my Pro Licence. He asked how much I would train the team, which I again found to be a strange question. He passed comment on the previous regime and seemed to think the team had not been training enough, that they only trained for an hour each day. I told him that in pre-season I would have plenty of double sessions, but that during the season itself it was usual to have just one session per day, given the proximity of matches. I told him the quality of sessions was just as important as the quantity.

I said I'd want to bring the team away in pre-season; I'd done it at Longford and it worked well for us. I spoke about strength and conditioning, but they said they already had someone (Cathal O'Shea) whom they were happy with.

They asked about players. I was anxious to bring Dave Mooney with me and I told them I could get him; I also wanted to bring Pat Sullivan. These were two of the best players at Longford.

Arkaga seemed keen to have me onboard, so I told them I'd be interested in the job, and confident of being able to take the position in a full-time capacity. My employers, Ulster Bank, had been very accommodating to allow me to participate in the League for many years and once again, when I asked them, they were very supportive. They were happy to let me take a leave of absence of three years (it was the time of the Celtic Tiger, remember), which was the timescale Arkaga were talking about. So it was all worked out, and on New Year's Eve 2007 I received an offer, in writing, which I was delighted to accept. I signed a three-year contract but I felt if things went well it could last even longer.

NH: So how did it go?

AM: I was welcomed in from the start. The players I found to be a good crew: Dan Murray, Colin Healy, Joe Gamble... great professionals, and lads you could talk to. While I was happy with pre-season, once the league began we seemed to have a difficulty keeping clean sheets – we kept giving away late goals – and I couldn't get my head around it. But when we finally got things sorted on the pitch we went on an unbelievable run, winning something like nine games in a row. Dave Mooney was on fire – he even set a goal-scoring record around Europe, scoring something like sixteen goals in nine consecutive games. We climbed to second or third in the league, and then we went to Finland.

NH: And then what happened?

AM: I was told the wages would be delayed. Pat Kenny – who had replaced Aidan Tynan as CEO – was the one who told me. I asked him why there was a delay but I wasn't happy with his response. I'd been suspicious of Pat since he came in; he seemed to be looking to make cutbacks left, right and centre, and putting pressure on me to make cutbacks. I didn't understand, until afterwards, where this was coming from – it was in direct opposition to what Arkaga had been indicating to me. In fact they'd put my mind at ease just before this trip to Finland.

NH: Why were you so concerned about Kenny?

AM: Pat Kenny's general demeanour didn't sit well with me. He seemed to be questioning everything I did and I was having arguments with him about little things. He wanted to know why we needed more training kit; why we needed a 54-seater bus; why we needed to charter a plane to Finland; why this cost and that cost... He was onto me about the cost of everything.

It seemed like I was an irritant to him, yet he'd been appointed by Arkaga. I couldn't see where this was coming from. I eventually had a falling-out with him and said something to which he replied, "That's no way to speak to a chief executive."

Up until this point I had tried my best to work with the man, for the sake of everybody, but when he said this I blew up and told him some home truths that didn't go down well.

I thought about it later that night when I was at home with my kids, and I realised something was wrong. I wouldn't have acted that way otherwise. So I decided to find out what was going on.

NH: What did you do?

AM: It was the mid-season break, but instead of catching a plane to Spain with my family I decided to let them go without me and I cancelled my ticket. You see, I needed to clarify what was going on. So I organised to meet with Gerard Walsh and I flew to London to see him.

I was collected at Heathrow by a chauffeur in a Bentley and I remember that the chauffeur wouldn't let me sit in the front with him.

"What are you doing?" he asked.

"I'll sit in the front with you."

"No, no – hop in the back," he said.

So I got in the back. It had deep pile carpets – totally luxury. As we were driving through London I saw the bullet-shaped Gherkin building and I remember feeling like I was in *The Apprentice*. Then we drove out of the city, off a slip-road, into the countryside and down a side lane. I thought, "I'm going to get shot here!"

We passed a lot of nice houses – big gates on each one – in some wealthy area outside of the city. Eventually we pulled up to a huge pair of brown gates and went through them, then up a long winding driveway, around a large roundabout with a fountain in the middle, and reached a house. The house reminded me of a miniature of the GPO – big columns everywhere. I'd say that house was on about 10,000 to 12,000 square feet of land, set back on a private wood of about 200 acres. A big estate indeed.

I was led into the drawing room where I met with Gerard Walsh, just beside a huge portrait of him that was hanging the length of the room. I was brought dinner and given a glass of wine. I told him I wanted to sign Gamble.

NH: Joe Gamble?

AM: Yes. I wanted to clear things up with the owner as to the direction we were going. That's why I was there. I felt if they signed Joe it would show they still had the same intentions they'd originally stated. Joe was being offered silly money by Pat's, but I wanted to keep him. I told Walsh that Georgy [O'Callaghan] was going back to England and that I wanted to utilise the budget in order to keep Joe, but Walsh didn't think

George would go. However, I'd already spoken with Ronnie Moore at Tranmere and they were keen to take him. Tranmere were due to play Liverpool live on Setanta TV and I felt this could swing it for Georgy, who would be happy anyway to move back to the UK.

Walsh agreed and I returned home on the last flight to sign Joe on a new deal, while Georgy was happy enough to go to Tranmere. This allayed my concerns somewhat before leaving for Finland.

Then, over in Helsinki, Pat Kenny told me about the delay with the wages. I was furious about it but decided to tell the players afterwards, when we'd returned home, as they needed to concentrate on the match. I was even more upset later as we were destroyed in that game, 4–0. We were horrific; I was gutted. But I told the lads to leave the result behind – to consider it an aberration and forget about it. When we got back to Cork I told them about the wages.

NH: What happened next?

AM: I remember we came back and beat Sligo, one-nil away, with Denis Behan scoring a lovely header. That was a great result – it showed real guts. Then we had Bohs at home: they were top of the league and the Cross that night was absolutely rocking. I remember thinking how brilliant it was... but we lost to a late Glen Crowe cross. We just switched off for a second and they scored. In truth I'd always felt it'd be in the second year that we'd have our best chance of winning the league, and even after that result we were still in with a shout – if we could keep our players.

NH: Who was the first to leave?

AM: Well, if you remember, we let David Meyler go for something like €100,000. He'd only played a handful of games with us – in fact he'd scored on his debut, over against a German side on the pre-season trip to Spain. I liked the kid; he had a contagious kind of humour about him and was a nice kid. He was always looking to improve his game and loved training. I liked his dad too. He used to come watch us training, I suppose with his added interest in being a GAA manager. They were good people. Others soon came looking for him. He was playing with the under-19 Irish side and Roy Keane and Niall Quinn at Sunderland were interested in him. He was 18 and anxious to go, and I wanted to give the guy a chance over there so we let him go. With his attitude and ability I thought he'd do well. Pat Kenny later said I'd let him go for too little, but he didn't see it from the footballing side of things. We weren't going to stand in his way, and with the add-ons that were included in the deal it was a good piece of business. But the story of what happened to those add-ons is for another day.

Later in the year when Reading came in for Mooney, Kenny said he would deal with it exclusively and that I was to stay away from the negotiations. So I spoke with their manager, Steve Coppell, and their Director of Football, Nicky Hammond, and I told them they had to go through Kenny. In the end I thought we should have gotten more for Mooney, but I suppose that's how it goes. After Mooney left we lost John O'Flynn, and then the wheels really started to fall off.

NH: But the team won the Setanta Cup?

AM: Yes, and that was really great considering everything that had gone on. It showed what we were capable of, even without the players that'd left. But had we kept those players until the end of the season, and added to them the next year, we would have been very successful. I believe we could have really progressed as we had a core of really good pros with great attitudes and lots of ability.

NH: It didn't turn out that way, though?

AM: No, it didn't. After examinership Tom Coughlan came in. From the start I felt he didn't know what he was doing. He told me he'd bought the pub; that he'd pay back the Deanrock (who I was very pleased with) and many other creditors... but he never did. He actually told me that he felt the team could be run by a committee – like in rugby – rather than by a manager. I felt undermined from the start but I didn't let it affect me. I fully intended to stay on because of the players we had, and because of the supporters, who were brilliant at getting behind the team.

Then, towards the end of the year, he invited me to the opening of the new club shop on Sullivan's Quay. We spoke about the coming year; he said we needed severe cutbacks to keep things going. He wasn't specific, only speaking in a general way. I outlined what I felt was required as a minimum to be successful the following season. However, we weren't agreeing on anything and in the end he walked off down the road without us coming to any agreement.

I received a call a few days later from him and he just said, "You're no longer manager of Cork City FC." This was despite the fact that I had two years left on my contract.

NH: What did you do?

AM: I contacted the League Managers' Association to tell them. I still hadn't been paid wages and was owed money for a good spell, about three months. Because of what had gone on over the months beforehand, it didn't come as much of a surprise to me. So I arranged to move out of the apartment near Mahon Point straight away (as the club was renting it) and to move back to Dublin. Jerry Kelly [the groundsman] called up to give me a hand when he heard. He was a great help throughout the season; he'd told me we needed an irrigation system at Bishopstown – sprinkles and a water tank. We put those in ourselves and it was the best money I ever spent, as Jerry soon had the pitch in perfect condition just about the time we went on our run. It really helped us on that run, I think. I'm still very appreciative of the work Jerry – and a lot of others – did for the club that year.

So Jerry helped me pack my stuff and bought me a pint. Billy Barry [local radio (96FM) DJ and Cork

City fan] then gave me a lift to the train station, saying he felt very bad about how I'd been treated. I got on the train and that was that.

NH: Looking back now, do you think your spell at Cork City was a missed opportunity?

AM: Yes and no. Personally, yes. And for the players, yes. We could have done some great things. But a professional League of Ireland is just not sustainable. You just have to look at our rugby friends and how they've done it. I went to watch Leinster in the RaboDirect last week: 15,000 people there. If soccer had a Leinster or a Munster and they were successful in Europe, you could get double that regularly. But it'll probably never happen. And unfortunately I don't see the league getting back to what it was between 2004 and 2008. With hindsight there was too much reliance on one person funding each club. Carroll at Boh's, Kelleher at St. Pat's, Ollie Byrne at Shels... On the other hand you look at Shamrock Rovers and see what one year's success in the Europa League brought them. The money's in Europe, but you need bigger teams to compete. The league's too fragmented, given our population, to survive as a full-time entity – especially given the competition from the GAA and rugby. I feel we will always be lagging behind.

~~~~~~~~~~~

Postscript

Alan Mathews was replaced in January 2009 by fellow Dubliner Paul Doolin, who had left the financially crippled Drogheda. However, the 2009 season was, in the end, to prove even more turbulent than 2008.

Despite most players agreeing to wage-cuts for the forthcoming season, funds emerged from somewhere for the signing of new players to bolster the squad. Consequently the team spent most of the early part season near the top end of the league. But while there were good results on the pitch, the players were to experience regular difficulties with wage payments throughout 2009. The High Court intervened in July as winding-up proceedings had been issued by the taxman – who, seemingly, had difficulties getting paid too.

With the club on the verge of extinction, businessman Dermot Desmond intervened, organising a match with Celtic FC which allowed for the last-minute reprieve of CCFC. The players continued to experience difficulties, however, with an event known as 'Busgate' (the bus driver refusing to transport the incumbent players to their away-match destination until payment of arrears had been made to his company) signifying a new low for the club.

Fans group FORAS, growing increasingly unhappy with events, announced that they were parting ways with chairman Tom Coughlan, who managed to see the club through until the end of the year. The team finished in an admirable third place and so achieved a Europa League spot (although subsequent events would cancel out the European place).

At the start of the following season (2010), Doolin was replaced by another Dubliner: Roddy Collins. This is where it all fell apart. Coughlan was charged by the FAI with bringing the game into disrepute; found guilty; fined €5,000 and suspended for 12 months from football-related activities. Around the same time FORAS called for Coughlan to step down and communicated the possibility of their members boycotting matches the following season.

Finally, following the failure of his High Court action to appeal his suspension by the FAI, Coughlan stepped down as Chairman in late January 2010. The FAI, unimpressed, issued a statement: *"Gestures at the eleventh hour when it could be too late to rectify next season are too little, too late."*

Not long after this the holding company of Cork City FC was liquidated. Reacting quickly, FORAS stepped into the breach, and having applied to enter a Cork City FC team for the 2010 season at short notice they were accepted by the League.

Under FORAS, the fans-owned Cork City FC scrambled to survive in the first division for a few years before marching into the Premier Division for the 2012 season under Tommy Dunne. At the time of writing (August 2014), John Caulfield – one of the guiding lights with whom the author played under Liam Murphy back in 2001 – has taken over as manager. Caulfield, the club's most capped player and joint-top scorer of all time, has wasted no time in galvanizing the club, bringing back full-capacity attendances to Turners Cross league games for the first time in a long time.

Some of the players of 2008 left to further their careers in more stable environments; of these, Kearney has returned, as have Crazy Daz, Healy and Dan Murray. Only last month the ever-electric John O'Flynn, who left in August of 2008, re-signed for City. Of the other players only McNulty and myself remain – albeit in a veteran capacity.

But a new breed of talented younger players have emerged and the club seems to be on the up once more. European qualification may even be on the horizon.

It would be nice to draw Bayern Munich...

Acknowledgements

Thank you to independent sportswriter Edward Newman for supporting the idea of this book from the very beginning. Thanks to Brian Lennox and Alan Mathews for finding the time to remember the past. Thanks to Stephen McGuinness and Ollie Cahill of the PFAI for your support. Thanks to the *Irish Examiner*, the *Irish Independent*, Extratime.ie, and the *Cork Independent* for kindly consenting to the reproduction of your articles. A particular thanks to Terry Reilly and the staff at the *Irish Examiner* for their help throughout the year. Thanks to Ciaran Buckley Barry at Urban Design and Print (www.urbanprint.ie) for the cover and for the help with the print version. Thanks to Paul Murray of wallwebdesign.ie for your impressive technical support. Thanks to Georgia Laval of www.lavalediting.co.uk for your criticism (nicely balanced with enthusiasm), your professionalism and, most of all, for your patience. Thanks to my colleagues, solicitors Gearoid McKernan and Dave Cowhey for their constructive advice and support. Thanks to Patrick O'Riordan B.L. for his advice. Thanks to the players, members, staff and fans of Cork City FC. Thanks to Mary, Tara, Patricia, Eoin and Caroline for putting up with it for so long.

Who's Who

Cork City Playing Staff, 2008

NAME	POSITION	NICKNAME
Alan Mathews	Team Manager	'The Gaffer'
Paul McGee	Assistant Manager	'Skee'
Phil Harrington	Goalkeeping Coach	'Biscuits'
Dan Murray	Captain/Defender	'Muzza/Muz'
Mick Devine	Goalkeeper	'Mick'
Mark McNulty	Goalkeeper	'Nults'
Sean Kelly	Defender	'Seany'
Neal Horgan	Defender	'Hoggie/Hogs'
Danny Murphy	Defender	'Murph'
Pat Sullivan	Defender	'Sully'
Darragh Ryan	Defender	'Daz'
Darren Murphy	Defender/Midfielder	'Crazy Daz'
Cillian Lordan	Defender/Midfielder	'Lordy'
Colin O'Brien	Midfielder	'Coly'
Billy Woods	Midfielder	'Woodsy'
Gareth Farrelly	Midfielder	'Gaz'
Joe Gamble	Midfielder	'No-Show Joe'

NAME	POSITION	NICKNAME
George O'Callaghan	Midfielder	'Georgy'
Colin Healy	Midfielder	'Healers'
Alan O'Connor	Midfielder/Forward	'Al'
Craig Duggan	Midfielder/Forward	'Craigy'
Denis Behan	Forward	'Denny'
John O'Flynn	Forward	'Flynny'
Tim Kiely	Forward	'Timmy'
Gareth Cambridge	Forward	
Dave Mooney	Forward	'Moons'
Lawrie Dudfield	Forward	
Alex Mason	Physio	
Dr Gerard Murphy	Club Doctor	'The Doc'
Jerry Harris	Secretary	
Jerry Kelly	Grounds Manager	
Éanna Buckley	Club Administrator	

sportsproview

www.sportsproview.com